STIMULUS OVERLOAD

Survival Manual

Jorjan Jane

Author's Tranquility Press
ATLANTA, GEORGIA

Jorjan Jane/Author's Tranquility Press
3900 N Commerce Dr. Suite 300 #1255
Atlanta, GA 30344, USA
www.authorstranquilitypress.com

Ordering Information:
Quantity sales. Special discounts are available on quantity purchases by corporations, associations, and others. For details, contact the "Special Sales Department" at the address above.

Stimulus Overload / Jorjan Jane
Hardback: 978-1-964810-92-8
Paperback: 978-1-964810-93-5
eBook: 978-1-964810-23-2

Contents

Stimulus Overload

Survival Manual

for teens and adults
who don't know they have it,
but put the pieces of the puzzle
together and find that . . .

It all adds up

JORJAN JANE

Are you frustrated, angry,
overwhelmed, forgetful and
confused?

Stop the madness!

Learn to recognize your problem,
understand why it occurs, and
discover ways to cope.

PREFACE

This book is about STIMULUS OVERLOAD. If you have this condition, you may have too many thoughts going on at the same time, bombarding you with so many options that you can't choose which thought takes precedence. You're revved up and ready to go, but your brain just short-circuited, leaving you unable to make the right move. You get upset because there is never enough time to do everything you need to do.

It's important for you to know this: It's not your fault.

Stimulus Overload comes from a chemical imbalance in the brain. As a result you end up confused, disorganized, and impulsive. You have a short attention span, are easily distracted, and can't finish what you started. You're frustrated because you're going in circles and getting nowhere. Others may think you're lazy or mentally slow. Not so.

The bad news is this condition can adversely affect your life.

The good news is that, just by realizing you're not flawed (even if you're a bit frazzled at times), you can lift the weight from your shoulders. Learning ways to cope will help you toss that weight into the trashcan for good.

I wrote this book because I too have struggled with Stimulus Overload. I have felt that weight on my shoulders. I want to help you understand and overcome your own struggles with Stimulus Overload so that you don't waste your life searching for answers.

If, after just five minutes of reading, I haven't convinced you that this book can change your life, then I've lost the challenge. And you already know a lot about challenge because that word— challenge—describes our entire existence.

I could suggest that you read this book sequentially from front to back, but that would be silly of me. My goal is for you to read the entire book in any way you can. The chapters have been written so you, the reader, can pick and choose the topic that suits you best at a given time.

In the first few chapters you'll find lists of traits associated with Stimulus Overload (which will be referred to as S.O. throughout most of the book). You may choose to read these chapters first. Or, if you're dealing with problems at your job or hoping to find a new job, you might find the information in Chapter Eight to be the best place to begin reading. If it's relationships that are your main concern, check out that chapter. For many of you, the most helpful part of the book will be the coping mechanisms, and the insight you gain from working with the questions at the end of the chapter.

This is your book, so go ahead and write on the pages. Make notes in the margins or at the end of the chapters. Highlight special phrases or things you want to remember. I know that if you lose interest, you won't pick this book up a second time. I can say that with certainty because I'm the same way. I encourage you to make this book a part of your life, because if you don't take the time to read it, you'll miss the chance to learn how to deal with your problems. You'll lose your chance to reach your full potential.

When all is said and done, my wish is for you to understand who you are and to feel good about that person. The best is yet to come!

ARE YOU A FRIEND OR FAMILY MEMBER?

If you don't suffer from Stimulus Overload yourself, it's almost impossible for you to understand the problems we experience on a daily basis, and it will also be hard for you to understand the impact this book may have on your friend or loved one's life.

Stimulus Overload is a bit like drowning and desperately grasping for that one last breath of air that will allow you to survive. Ordinary things are often overwhelming. Certain situations such as high noise levels can cause us to react and pull away, instinctively trying to avoid mental pain and frustration in the same way someone would pull away from a flame to keep from being burned.

We get confused or forgetful, and you wonder why we just can't get it together. The truth is, we have, but we forgot what we did with it.

You can help by being our coach or cheerleader, by giving us pep talks to motivate us. When we react with anger, run with us. When we're stressed, give us space, but please don't give up on us. Realize that we have many skills and hidden talents. When we finally make up our minds to do something, it's full speed ahead and the sky is the limit.

WHO CAN BENEFIT FROM THIS BOOK

* Those who feel overwhelmed, angry, and confused most of the time

* Those who have had a drastic or sudden change in their lives

* Those who work with the difficult, rebellious, and sometimes unreachable person but don't understand the reasons behind that behavior (aside from thinking

the person needs a swift kick in the butt)

- Teachers

- Parents

- Employers

- Ministers

- Police Officers

- Judges

- Probation Officers

- Legislators

- Social Workers

- Doctors

- Marriage Counselors, Therapists, etc.

Stimulus Overload occurs without regard to race, class, age, or intelligence. Sufferers include

- Movie Stars

- Musicians

- Geniuses

- Death Row Inmates

- Athletes

- Artists

- Race Car Drivers

- Firemen

- Jet Pilots

- Doctors

- Carjackers

- Bull Riders

- Soldiers

This list could go on indefinitely, but you get the picture. Stimulus Overload doesn't care who you are or what you do.

Please note: Stimulus Overload is not a medical diagnosis. It is a condition brought on by a short circuit in the brain. This is sometimes triggered by overwhelming circumstances such as stress, looming deadlines, divorce, death, accidents, threats, or simply problems dealing with life.

It shouldn't be considered a label or have negative connotations. Various traits can mimic or actually be one of the following: dyslexia, attention deficit disorder (ADD) with or without hyperactivity, depression, bi-polar disorder, post-traumatic stress disorder, or obsessive compulsive disorder (OCD).

HOLD HARMLESS AGREEMENT

I am not a doctor. I am someone who has suffered from Stimulus Overload myself, and as a result, I have learned to cope with the multitude of problems that this condition presents. I'm sharing this information in the hope that you can avoid some of the pitfalls in your life by using these coping mechanisms.

After reading this book, if you go out and set the world on fire (so to speak), don't blame me for your fame and fortune. You are responsible and you deserve all the credit.

DEDICATION

I have written this book for my sons, grandchildren, and greatgrandchildren, all of who suffer from various forms of Stimulus Overload. It is a genetic trait that I have passed on to them.

I could say it's unfortunate, but I won't. Despite all the drawbacks, there is a pot of gold at the end of the rainbow. May they learn to rise above the storm with their exceptional insights and talents.

My husband knows how difficult it can be to live with someone with Stimulus Overload. It can be a real challenging experience. I thank him for all the years of love and perseverance.

And a special thanks goes to my parents.

First, to my Mom, for her strict upbringing, for teaching me good work ethics, for showing me how to make something from nothing, and for passing her creative talents on to me.

Second, to my Dad, with his Irish humor and laughter to get through the tough times. He taught me humility, manners, how to be a social butterfly, and to always look for the best in everyone.

WHO IS JORJAN JANE?

I grew up in Batavia, Ohio, a small Midwestern town with strong family ties and community values. At age three I began dancing lessons, and at fourteen I joined the ballet corps in the Cincinnati summer opera. My independent streak displayed itself early as I worked and lived away from home during the summer.

Although I attended Cincinnati College of Music for ballet and the University of Cincinnati Teachers College, I became restless and eventually put my education on hold so that I could go to New York and follow my dream. My passion was ballet, but after working for several years in ballet companies, living below the poverty level, I moved west, to Las Vegas, to dance in the big extravaganza on the Las Vegas Strip *(Hello America* at the Desert Inn and *Casino de Paris* at the Dunes).

In a major change of direction, I gave up dancing on the Strip and began patrolling it instead when I was hired as one of the first women police officers in patrol. Over the years I worked as an operations coordinator at McCarran Airport, inspecting runways and handling bomb threats, hijackings, emergency landings, and plane crashes. Along the way I worked as a motivational therapist, hypnotist, and graphologist.

I have always been a perpetual student. My insatiable appetite for learning has turned each subject of study into the foundation for interest in another, and I never stop yearning to know more. I have degrees in five different fields: psychology, sociology, criminal justice, art, and communications. I graduated from the University of Nevada, Las Vegas, doing my graduate work at the University of Humanistic Studies. I interned with Dr. Eva von Rheinwald.

For eight years I worked two jobs while I went to school in my spare time. I also served as chief cook and bottle washer at home and raised two sons while attending political functions with my husband. As union steward at the airport, I negotiated contracts for county employees.

This book is based not only on my personal experience as someone with Stimulus Overload and other overlapping traits, but also as a mother and grandparent with children who suffer from the same problems. In addition, as a police officer, I've seen the devastating effects of internal rage and the destructive path taken by people out of control due to the effects of Stimulus Overload.

My experience as a motivational consultant and crisis counselor helped me learn to cope with stress and feelings of being overwhelmed, and I have shared those insights with others. Using hypnosis as a valuable tool, I've helped Stimulus Overload sufferers to bypass the negativity and low self-esteem, thereby allowing them to focus on their talents instead.

Because I've been lucky enough to travel the world, I've been exposed to many cultures and peoples of varied ethnic backgrounds. People worldwide are looking for answers to their confusion, frustration, and inability to move ahead. I find this especially true in countries where alcoholism and drug abuse is rampant.

AS I LIVE AND BREATHE—MY PERSONAL EXPERIENCE WITH STIMULUS OVERLOAD

As a child I was a very determined girl who didn't know the word *defeat.* If I couldn't figure out how to do something, I got angry and threw a temper tantrum. I'd kick, scream, and slam doors. I'd wear myself out, and then fall asleep. When I awoke, I couldn't remember being angry and went back to solving the problem at hand. My mother, in her infinite wisdom, enrolled me in dancing lessons, knowing I could work off some of my excess energy in a constructive way.

At home I was the errand girl. Mom would ask me to go to the grocery store before it closed in five minutes, knowing I could run fast. I'd leave the house like a starter gun had fired, and the race was on. I'd arrive two minutes before the store closed, but couldn't remember what I was supposed to buy. It seemed like I could only concentrate on one thing at a time, and my speed—the race to get to the store—blanked out anything Mom had said after the word *hurry.*

As I grew older, I learned to hate the word *hurry.* That little word became a thorn in my side. It sent me into a panic, blocking out everything else, taking away my concentration. I can't count the times I wrecked my bike. Once I rode in front of a car without looking, simply because I was trying to accomplish something in a specific time frame.

School and college presented very real challenges. I took at least five to six times longer than the average person to understand what I had read. I was forced to read my assignments over and over before anything made sense. Always fearful I'd omit some important fact, I'd take detailed notes. Then I'd write a summary of my notes and go back and highlight that summary.

During lectures my notes looked like a mad man's diary. I wrote up, down, sideways along the page, drew pictures in the margins, and added insightful thoughts or parodies that popped into my mind. Many of these had nothing to do with the topics. I'd switch from pen to pencil when the subject changed.

I tried so hard to get the facts to sink in, but I often thought I must be retarded. My brain seemed to shut down and I'd miss several minutes of the lecture. Don't misunderstand me. Despite the problems, my persistence and hard work was not without rewards.

Teachers often praised me on a job well done. I needed—no, I craved —that constant reassurance. My grade point average proved I wasn't dumb although I still secretly thought I was because it took me so long to understand the material. On exam days I was a nervous wreck. I would get so tense that I'd hyper focus (go into extreme concentration) out of fear of failing. At the time, however, I didn't know what hyper focus meant or how it kicked in.

When fellow students would ask what I got on the test, I'd respond that it was a difficult exam or that I'd stayed up all night studying and still missed some questions. When they asked again what grade I'd gotten, I would sheepishly say ninety-six. Their indignant and flippant response of "Oh yeah, you really thought it was hard!" made me furious. If they only knew how damn hard I had studied, how many nights I'd stayed up to read and re-read the assignments. If they had put in only one-tenth of the time I did, they too would have gotten a good grade.

Nothing ever came easy. I earned everything the hard way. I had to. It was totally unacceptable for me to be less than perfect, but that was another problem. I was never content and was always in competition with myself.

As an adult, things didn't get easier. When I worked as the operations coordinator at the airport, meetings were grueling because new policies would be passed around for us to read and make comments. I not only can't read fast, but when I'm under pressure, I can't read at all. Frustration built from the confusion and I constantly feared someone would discover my secret.

How was I to understand the context when I was only staring at the words, feeling like an illiterate because I didn't have the foggiest idea what the words meant. I could get the gist of the memo by the comments others made, and then I'd adlib when I was called upon. In an emergency, however, I could function well because I'd go into a hyper focus mode. The same held true when I was a police officer because it was often a life or death situation, which automatically caused me to hyper focus and to clearly and quickly revert back to instincts and training.

I could win an Academy Award for some of the performances I pulled off over the years. Most people suffering from Stimulus Overload and Attention Deficit Disorder could. The sad thing is, I always felt like a fake —you know the feeling, I'm sure—but I really wasn't.

An exhaustive schedule kept me too tired to worry. I was busy working two jobs, going to college, and fulfilling my internship requirement with a psychologist. In addition, I was running a household, raising my sons, playing chauffeur to soccer games and wrestling matches, and being a cheerleader for the kids. I also filled the role of family correspondent, bill payer, cook, and wife. Boy, was I tired!

I rarely slept, averaging only about fifteen hours of sleep a week with the exception of Fridays and Mondays. On those days I didn't sleep at all. In order to fit everything into my schedule, I simply forfeited two days of rest. My choice was between being uptight or rummy, and it was much easier choosing physical exhaustion than to suffer from mental fatigue. Being tired was much better than having all that energy and using it to fuel anger and frustration.

One hot August day, after getting off a twelve-hour shift, I stopped at the grocery store on my way home. When I pulled into the driveway, I thought I'd grab a quick ten-minute nap by leaning over the steering wheel. Instead I fell asleep for an hour, with temperatures soaring to one hundred fifteen degrees. When I woke, the ice cream was soup, the milk was hot, the frozen foods were defrosted, but surprisingly the eggs weren't hard-boiled and the popcorn hadn't popped.

As much as I wanted to go to bed—as much as I craved more sleep—I couldn't. I needed to bake a cake for my son's birthday.

Any change or slip-up in my routine threw me totally off course. I'd try to fit in as much time with the kids as possible, even if it meant giving up more sleep, but there was never enough time with them to suit me. I felt stretched to the limit, like a rubber band about to snap.

With the addition of noise or annoying sounds, I'd be unable to think straight. At the library, sitting next to someone clicking a pen, I'd nearly go berserk. It would take every bit of energy I could summon to keep from grabbing the offending pen and throwing it as far as possible. Or taking someone's cell phone away when they were rude enough to make a call and talk loudly. These behaviors caused me to react with anger. I was unable to block them out, so I'd have to leave.

When I decided to write a book to help others suffering from Stimulus Overload, the question was, could I stick with it? Initially I found myself getting off on one tangent and then another, but I kept pulling myself back to the main topic. After seeing my progress, I was pleased. I wrote the book in three weeks, but as I was basking in my accomplishment, I accidentally hit the wrong button on the computer. Every single word I'd written was wiped out and I had no backup. Do you remember when I said *nothing* is easy for us?

I have always had to learn everything the hard way.

I must have stared at the computer for an hour. I couldn't believe what had happened. I had to restrain myself from throwing the computer out the window, and for several months I cussed under my breath every time I walked past my desk.

Then one remarkable day, I gathered my wits and sat down in front of the computer. I'd remembered a lot of what I had written and more began coming back. Once I got rolling again, I couldn't stop and I didn't stop, not to eat, not to pee, not even to sleep. I finished the book and celebrated. Yippee! Yahoo!

Of course, as any writer knows, rewrites are often harder than first drafts and I had to rewrite a few choppy chapters. I'd write, type, rewrite, retype, and then think of something else to add. I ended up redoing the entire book three times.

In many areas, my lack of computer skills had stymied me. I signed up for computer classes, but it would be months before I was proficient. Too time consuming, I thought, I'm going to go nuts. I was so disgusted that I didn't go near the computer again for a year. I gave myself pep talks, but they didn't help.

When I'm frustrated about something, I have to block it out, because if I dwell on it, it renders me useless. One day, however, the answer hit me like a bolt of lightning. Why hadn't I hypnotized myself? That would have been my advice to someone else with the same problem, but I hadn't applied it to me.

Mission accomplished. I won't let disappointments knock me on my butt again (at least not this week).

NOTES:

CHAPTER 1

TRAITS-CHECKLIST

Everyone has some of the traits listed below, but if you identify with the majority of them, you might have Stimulus Overload (S.O.). By the time you've completed this checklist, you will either feel this exercise has pinpointed your problem, or you'll know it doesn't have much bearing at all.

What you do with the information is up to you. If you think you're out of control and need medication, seek professional help. We all have choices in life and you must decide what is best for you. Although I've never taken medication for S.O., there have been times in my life when it would have helped.

CHECKLIST OF TRAITS ASSOCIATED WITH STIMULUS OVERLOAD

________ Inability to focus on consequences

________ Difficulty concentrating

________ Easily distracted

________ Very sensitive to rejection, teasing, and criticism

________ Continually forgetting important dates, deadlines, and calls

________ Tendency to take on too many tasks

________ Problems with time management (how long does it take to finish a particular job) Fails to finish projects

________ Doesn't listen to an entire conversation (starts drifting)

________ Acts quickly before thinking (leaps before he looks)

________ Impatient

________Disorganized lifestyle (late, rushed, or unprepared)

________ Interrupts others

________ Tends to blame others

________ Fidgets and can't sit still

________ Moves excessively during sleep

________ Extremist (gets either overwhelmed or hyper with stimuli)

________ Inconsistent

________ Difficulty managing a checkbook or finances Drinks excessively or binges (now or in prior years) Takes drugs (now or previously) Gets lost easily

________ Misplaces keys continually and loses things

________ Any minor change in plans becomes upsetting

________ Rebellious, aggressive, or volatile

________ Poor study skills

________ Depressed

________ Feels incomplete no matter how successful

________ Problems with the law ________ Hard to soothe or hold

________ Irregular eating habits and/or too much junk food eaten

________ Lives on the edge, a thrill seeker

________ Creative

________ Comedian

________ Low self-esteem

________ High level of awareness

________ Daydreamer

________ Soulful

_________ Can go without sleep for long periods of time

_________ Can hyper focus to finish something if there's a dire need

_________ Fast mood changes

_________ Low tolerance level

_________ Slow to mature, responsibility wise

_________ Dyslexic

_________ Can be a whiz kid at video games or computers

_________ Withdrawn, prefers living in own little world

_________ Has piles of paperwork, books, and junk stacked everywhere

_________ Accident prone, runs into things, pinches fingers, bumps head

Ambidextrous Problem gambler Defiant

_________ Frequent headaches, stomachaches and vomiting Messy bedroom

_________ Multiple marriages or significant others Pack rat, saves everything

_________ Won't be around someone who talks too much Likes big cities

_________ Falls asleep when bored (especially in class) Enjoys working with hands

_________ Overly sensitive to smells, taste, sounds, touch, and sight Picky-picky

_________ Extremely neat or extremely sloppy (no in between) Entrepreneur

_________ Difficulty in finding the right words to explain something

_________ Constant nibbler

_________ Struggles to be a perfectionist

_______ Empathy for others
_______ Difficulty following instructions
_______ Makes numerous lists but loses them.
_______ Often on a different wave length than others

NOTES:

CHAPTER 2

YOU MIGHT HAVE STIMULUS OVERLOAD IF ...

Have you ever heard of Jeff Foxworthy? He's the comedian with the routine that begins "You might be a redneck if . . ." We all need to be able to laugh at ourselves from time to time, which is why I've titled this chapter, "You might have Stimulus Overload if . . ."

Do any of these statements make you nod your head in agreement? Are you laughing because you did one of these things yesterday or because someone you know made a similar comment about you or your home?

- You change your clothes two or three time before leaving the house.

- A cuckoo clock drives you stark raving mad.

- Someone makes a snide remark to you and you want to slap the crap out of him.

- The outside of your house and garage looks like the Sanford and Son junkyard.

- You've read the manual three times and still can't figure out how to set the VCR (your next step is to throw it on the floor and stomp it to death).

- Restraining yourself from a confrontation takes more energy than the fight itself.

- You flip yourself out of a hammock.

- You have even flipped a rocking chair over backwards.

• You think you're a scatterbrain or space cadet.

• You wonder if you were dropped on your head as a baby.

• You are rushed for time, someone keeps repeating *hurry up,* and you lose it.

• Someone tells you to settle down and you go ballistic.

• You wonder if a sixteen-year-old can get Alzheimer's disease.

• You left the laundry in the washer until it mildewed.

• You can't figure out that last word, *mil-dew-ed.*

• You can live for a week off the stuff in your fanny pack purse.

• You can't go to sleep, because there's a fly in the bedroom.

• You have to lean against the cupboard doors to close them.

• You have stockpiled enough emergency supplies to last through two wars, an earthquake, and a tornado.

• You start out on vacation from Ohio and head to Florida, but you end up in Michigan.

• Every day is a bad hair day.

• The smell of a pig farm makes you gag.

• You let your alligator mouth override your hummingbird ass.

• You come home from the store and put the milk in the cupboard and your keys in the refrigerator.

- You just went to the store for dog food, but you came back with a carload of groceries and still no dog food.

- You are overwhelmed by power bumps when you have to reset all the blinking clocks, phone recorder, microwave, sprinkler timer, TV, VCR, and computer.

- Someone has to perform the Heimlich maneuver on you to get you breathing again after barely making a deadline.

- You can't tell which side is up on a road map.

- You gave up a game of croquet to ride the mechanical bull at Gilly's.

- You forgot to wear a bra when you went bungee jumping.

- It's April 15th, 11:59 P.M., and you just mailed your tax return to the IRS . . .

If many of these statements apply to you and your life, then you might have Stimulus Overload.

NOTES:

CHAPTER 3

WHY IT OCCURS

Stimulus Overload occurs when there's a short circuit in the brain. It's much like a power outage. Sometimes a thought or action can't be completed because there's a gap in the sequence of events. This is often due to a chemical imbalance in the body.

The problem of S.O. seems to be passed on genetically, especially if one of the parents drank heavily, took drugs, or suffered from depression. However, none of these need be the case.

It's not my fault—it's not your fault—that the brain stops functioning from time to time. It's just the way the cards were dealt. Some people have low blood sugar and get dizzy if they don't eat at regular intervals. Others have poor eyesight and must wear glasses. Still others suffer from high blood pressure and must keep it under control to avoid having a stroke and being left paralyzed.

There are certain things everyone has to do to continue to function. Since no one is perfect, no one is exempt. Everyone has problems. Some of these are big, some are small, but *everyone* has to deal with problems. Herein lies the difficulty.

If the symptoms are barely noticeable, they are shrugged off. By the time we're spinning out of control, it's too late. Therefore, it's important to plan ahead.

When planning a party, for example, it's common to buy a little extra food in case extra people show up. When preparing for a vacation, it's normal to save a little extra money to cover those unexpected items and to pack an additional outfit for weather changes. If there were lots of errands to run, no one would leave home without making sure there's enough gas in the car.

Someone with S.O. *must* plan ahead for the inevitable, and that inevitable is that we *can't think.* We don't always know when a problem is going to occur, but when it does, our brains shut down. That leaves us running around like a chicken with its head cut off. Although the body is physically responding, we're going in circles and getting nowhere.

The cause might be a stressful audit by the IRS or a death in the family, but no matter what has triggered the shutdown, we temporarily don't know what to do. One minute we're fine, but the next we're out of commission. There might as well be a sign around our necks, reading, "Out to lunch—Be back soon."

I could be walking down the street when an attractive person runs up, grabs me, and gives me a big kiss. Although I may keep walking, my mind is flooded with a multitude of options. Should I turn around and say, "Thank you, I needed that!" Should I yell, "Get lost, you pervert!" Or should I say, "Come back and give me your name and phone number. This could be the start of something grand."

That particular situation is pure fiction, but it helps me to dream up various situations that might occur and think about how I would handle them.

Unfortunately when you have S.O., you often try to anesthetize yourself with alcohol, diet pills, or cocaine. You instantly feel smarter and more organized because the alcohol or drugs help rein in your racing mind. You don't drink or take drugs to get high. You do it to slow down and focus (although I wouldn't try telling this to a judge).

It's a double bind. The very substances you think are helping are only making you worse in the long run. The craving for a fix could come from an endorphin deficiency (a chemical imbalance). Your goal is to feel good and be able to think clearly.

Dopamine is a substance that's involved in the feeling of pleasure. Think of it like dope. We all need dopamine in our brain to feel good. We aren't producing enough neurotransmitters in the brain so we don't have the proper chain reaction to finish a thought. Stimulant drugs or medications like Ritalin increase the level of neurotransmitters, allowing us to connect the dots (synapses).

Even smoking cigarettes is a form of self-medication. I smoked for years to calm my nerves. Why does it work? Because it increases the dopamine, which in turn increases the firing of neurons in the brain. That also explains why quitting was so difficult. I became both physically and psychologically used to the calming effects.

Like you, I'm mesmerized by the external world and everything that's going on around me. I can't stop the input, which results in an inability to concentrate. And, as though that isn't enough, there are impulses. I'll try not to get too technical, but bear with me. This is important.

The frontal lobe region of the brain is the major regulator of behavior. It keeps our impulses in check. When it goes awry or if we've had an injury to that part of the brain, we lose the ability to apply the brakes. This explains why we can't learn from past mistakes and instead keep repeating them. We don't have the ability to be conditioned with either praise or punishment because of our neurological system. We can't stay with a task until it's finished because we're biologically predisposed. We're constantly bombarded with other stimulus (unless we're playing Nintendo and hyper focusing).

The problem can't be blamed on bad parenting. The culprit is heredity.

I know it's not nice to fool Mother Nature, but with Stimulus Overload we need to know how to connect the synapses (circuits) naturally (without medication, if possible) if they won't bridge the gap.

One way is to get more oxygen to the brain by breathing deeply. Another way to connect the circuits is to get highly motivated with a strong drive and passion to accomplish something. This will help us hyper focus. A third way is through high-risk behavior because it releases adrenaline to the brain like a stimulant medication. This has become a way of life for those who chose a risk-taking career. It is the uncertainty the bull rider feels when the chute opens. It is the rush the policeman feels driving code with red lights and siren to a robbery in progress. It is the compulsion the firefighter feels as he runs back into the burning building to save a child. It is the fear, the excitement, and the unknown all rolled into one. unfortunately the use of drugs and alcohol are another way to fool Mother Nature. These will only have a temporary effect and may cause a lifetime of misery and addiction.

Stimulus Overload is like a reward deficiency. This is why some of us become workaholics. We're searching for gratification, looking for validation that we're worthwhile.

Remember though, we only feel successful for a short time before beginning to search for another way to prove our worth. Success is a fleeting fantasy, here one minute and gone the next. We become driven and frustrated. We're not only marching to the sound of a different drummer, but we're marching out of step because the neurons in the brain are misfiring.

We're not only out of sync, it's likely we're in a different parade altogether.

None of these problems are new. There have always been people with a chemical imbalance in the brain or shorts in their electrical system. It seems more prevalent today, however, because most of us live life in the fast lane. We rush off to school or to work without eating properly. We're tense and uptight all day due to the increased stress of modern technology —the very things often touted as timesavers. Computers crash. Deadlines loom. Ultimatums are handed down.

In addition, with less manual labor to perform, we're unable to work off our frustration. The majority of us don't get enough exercise or fresh air. We leave work, stop for a few drinks, or ingest drugs to unwind and slow down after a hectic day. More mothers are working, adding the burden of finding good childcare facilities. The stress of leaving teenagers alone to fend for themselves can be tremendous. There's a rush from the time the children get up until they leave for school, and it begins again in the afternoon when you're hurrying to pick them up on time and get a nutritious meal on the table. Taking time off work to deal with parent-teacher conferences or taking your children to the doctor or dentist adds another layer of stress.

Children watch too much television so their role models become wrestlers on steroids, sexy teenyboppers with no visible moral standards, or soap opera queens having daily affairs. Think about their heroes, the tattooed athletes with poor sportsmanship qualities and the talk show hosts who allow their guests to be rude, interrupt, and run amuck. You can see why children as well as adults no longer have respect for other people's feelings, opinions, or space, let alone respect for themselves.

When we're driven by someone else's standards, our lifestyle becomes overwhelming. You've heard the saying "going to hell in a hand basket." Well, sometimes I feel it's true.

There's so much—too much—divorce, bankruptcy, abuse, and suicide. There's a lack of responsibility that stretches from not paying bills on time to getting to work late. The workplace has become dog-eat-dog.

There's an abundance of dishonesty and a lack of spirituality. There's too much violence and not enough love. Too many people think only of themselves and of what they want. Too many people try to force their opinions on others, but they don't realize it's rare to change someone's mind through a violent act or insult.

In addition to the worry of job layoffs, over-extended credit, and threats of war, we now have terrorism to add to the mix. It's a huge threat to our peace of mind. There's a lot going on in this stressful life, and it will only get worse if we don't find ways of coping and planning ahead.

It's up to us.

It's time to step up to the bat and take responsibility for our own lives.

Wouldn't you rather be admired for your strength than pitied for your weakness? (And did I mention that another trait of Stimulus Overload is going off on a tangent?)

The brain is huge—inside it is held a heaven and a hell.

—Oscar Wilde

GLOSSARY

Adrenaline: A hormone that is released into the bloodstream in response to stress. It makes the heart pound, raises blood pressure, increases blood sugar, and increases the metabolic rate.

Dopamine: One of the chemicals that communicates messages between nerve cells. Most of the nerve cells in the pleasure center of the brain are activated when there is increased brain activity of dopamine. An abnormality leads to an impaired ability to achieve a sense of well-being.

Endorphin: The body's natural painkiller, endorphins help create a sense of well-being.

Frontal Lobe: Front portion of the brain, which controls emotional responses and social judgment.

Neurotransmitters: Chemical messengers released from nerve endings when electrically stimulated.

ASK YOURSELF

1. What activities give you a rush of adrenaline?
2. What stresses you the most?
3. Who stresses you the most?
4. Can you recall the last two times you seemed to run around incircles, unable to get going in the right direction? When did this occur? Why? Was it due to an emotional state or something else? Hunger? Exhaustion?

NOTES:

CHAPTER 4

COPING MECHANISMS

GET PHYSICAL

Run, dance, swim, play basketball, play volleyball, ride a bicycle, play golf, go mountain climbing, spar with a punching bag, go skating or skateboarding, dig in the garden, ride a horse, head to the go-kart track, ride a roller coaster, jump rope. Do something physical.

IF YOU'RE IN A RUT, DO WHAT I DO

Give yourself a pep talk, sing an upbeat song, learn a Tibetan mantra, take a yoga class, say three Hail Mary's, buy some worry beads (and use them), be hypnotized, shout out military cadence, write down your blessings.

MAKE YOUR LIFE EASIER

Get a phone recorder or voice mail. Buy a "Do Not Disturb" sign, Hide-A-Key containers, key finders (a device to locate your keys when you clap your hands), a kitchen timer, sticky notes, pocket notebooks, a PDA or electronic organizer, correction fluid, In/Out baskets, files, labels, colored pens and highlighters, a worry stone, ear plugs, an eye mask.

FOR A CHANGE OF PACE OR AN EMOTIONAL
OUTLET

Take music lessons, go fishing, enroll in an art class, sign up for baseball, coach a soccer team, answer phones for a hotline, take dancing lessons, learn a foreign language, write down your thoughts in a journal, take a sewing or cooking class, have a massage, read a good book, go to a movie, take a woodworking class, learn flower arranging.

OTHER IDEAS FOR COPING

• Ask a close trusted friend to be your coach or cheerleader to help and encourage you to reach your goals.

• Have a brainstorming session with yourself or with friends.

• Eat right and take a multivitamin every day.

• Accentuate the positive and eliminate the negative. Life is like the boomerang. What you throw out will come right back to you.

• Keep a calendar listing important events: doctor's appointments, court dates, vacation requests, sick leave, birthdays, football games, seminars.

• Keep photo albums up to date. Write down the names of the people in the photo, where it was taken, and the date. Get someone to help you put this all together. Make it an interesting evening. Order a pizza and have fun.

• Memorize as much as you can: your credit card numbers, phone numbers, addresses, and zip codes. This will save a lot of aggravation when you need the information and can't find it.

• Never wait until the last minute to do your taxes, write a term paper, or fill out a loan application. Complete tasks like these right away. You never know when there will be an emergency and you'll have to leave town. What would happen if you were injured and couldn't get to the task for three months? The thought of what you need to do, but haven't, bugs you every single day until you find yourself running around in circles at the last minute on the verge of a panic attack. At this point you're unable to think clearly enough to get the job done.

• Play tapes of environmental sounds like waves, the wind, birds, and wind chimes. Lose yourself in the music that you enjoy most.

• Find quiet time to recharge your batteries (soak in the tub or take a shower). Find a private sanctuary even if it's just a little corner or cupboard to call your own. You need a quiet place where you can think, dream, or relax without interruptions even if the peace and quiet only lasts fifteen minutes.

• Break down a big job into short, one-hour segments. Do some today and some tomorrow, and before you know it, the job will be done. It's like having a car payment for three years, and you've paid on it for two years and ten months. Little by little you've been working toward the completion of the payments. Think of each chore as a payment; if you don't follow through, being close doesn't count.

• Delegate the job or hire someone to do it for you just to get it done. There are three ways to look at a project. Remember: Do it, Delegate it, or Ditch it.

• If possible, trade off with a friend to do what you are more inclined to do. Realize that you can't be Super Mom, Super Dad, Super Mechanic. When you take on too much, the quality of your work goes downhill. Haven't you been in a doctor's office where there are ten patients ahead of you (too many patients, too little time)?

• Learn to say no. "No, I can't take care of the kids on Saturday because I've set aside that day to clean house." "No, I can't talk right now because I'm in the middle of a project." "No, I can't visit today; I'm trying to get the bills paid before the mailman comes." "No, I can't loan you twenty dollars until payday". Others don't care about your priorities, so it's up to you to set limits or others will usurp your time. Never forget that time is a precious commodity. Sometimes you have to be selfish, and rather than making someone else's life easier, make your own life easier. Consider making an appointment with a credit counselor or a financial advisor to get your money matters in line. Paperwork like this isn't pleasant, but it is necessary. Don't feel sorry for every charity that wants a donation. You are so good-hearted that you'll give until you have nothing left. Organizations love you because you give impulsively. Remember the old adage: Charity begins at home.

Avoid gambling. Because I live in Las Vegas, I can't fail to mention gambling and its devastating effects on people and marriages. The casinos and resorts build new high rises each year, bigger and better, and they are doing this with *your* hard-earned money. When you gamble, you continue to make the casino owners and corporations richer.

When you gamble, you're handing them your paycheck as though they need it more than you. Most of you don't gamble as a form of entertainment. Instead you go overboard, chasing a fool's dream. It's addicting. It taunts and teases by letting you win a few bucks. It entices you to play more, to win big. You feel you're just dollars away from that big jackpot.

Why risk your money on false hopes? There's no skill involved in gambling. Winning is random luck. Gambling addictively doesn't create character. It reveals it. You want something for nothing and gambling may be your drug of choice. It can give a temporary high, but next month you could be sleeping in a box by the railroad tracks. It's not worth it.

Gambling reminds me of the great expectations of mistletoe with green foliage and white berries all tied with a pretty red bow, placed in a spot where you must walk under it. It creates the anticipation of something wonderful (a kiss), but how soon we forget that mistletoe is a parasite and a fungus disguised in pretty packaging for marketing. Is gambling any different?

• Have a plan or you will waste too much time going around incircles. When you don't have a specific plan, you will head in too many directions—all at the same time. You need to achieve something to get you on a roll. If you have five different projects planned, finish one to give you the incentive to complete the others. Work is good when it's structured and has some order to it.

• Build your assets. Experiences are gradual, but they accumulate over time like interest in the bank. Improve your talents, education, and relationships. A seed planted today doesn't sprout tomorrow. Take a conversational Spanish class, a course in calligraphy, or a class on computers.

• Exercise. It increases deep breathing and gets more oxygen to the brain to help you think better. If you can't fit exercise into your schedule, do it while watching television. Sit on the floor and stretch. Jump up and run in place during commercials. Life is nothing but an obstacle course so you better be in good shape to clear all the hurdles.

• Learn to relax. Trying to relax or go to sleep at night

is like turning off the engine of an old car. Sometimes it continues to run, a condition called dieseling. It pings and knocks for a while, then finally shuts down. Bad timing causes this problem; a valve that is electronically controlled has malfunctioned. It is no different than the S.O. mind, which is controlled electronically and won't always shut off. This is why S.O. sufferers are so restless in bed.

• Have a contingency plan. Keep a notebook of things to do in case of a power outage, a wreck, a fire, etc. If a thought preys on your mind, then it's worth writing it down and finding a solution. If you can't think of a solution, ask a friend or co-worker what they would do in that same situation. If you panic when something occurs, you won't be able to think straight. It's advisable to have your handy, dandy notebook ready with emergency steps to follow. Add to it from time to time. List the topics you want to address: what steps you would take if you were transferred out of town, how you would pay bills if you lost your job.

What would you need to do prior to a month-long hospital stay?

Know your limits. How much can you drink without getting drunk (before a meal, after a meal)? How much can you buy without overspending or going into debt (ten dollars extra each month or . . .)? How much can you eat without putting on five pounds (ice cream and cake every night or only once a week as a special treat)? How much harassment can you take before you unravel? Mood and Mode. If someone is trying to teach you something and you are not in the learning mode, you will not grasp the facts. The same is true of the creative mode or the work mode. Your mood and your mode go hand in hand with the gear that your brain is in, like it or not. The average person finds this hard to believe, but we simply cannot function until we clearly focus on the job at hand and this has nothing whatsoever to do with self-discipline. If you're unable to think clearly, don't try to pay bills or do anything that requires mental alertness. Do something physical instead. Clean your bathroom, wash your car, or do the dishes. Don't try to do something you're not geared to do at that particular time.

During the day we switch back and forth from right brain functioning to left brain functioning, and this doesn't always occur at the most opportune times. We have to go with the flow or it's much like trying to get a crab to walk a straight line. It can't do it.

A friend told me that as creative as she is, there was no way she could have her own business because not every day is a creative one. 'I'd be in big trouble if I had to create something on demand. That's just not the way my mind works." The right side of the brain is the creative side while the left is the analytical half. That's why you can't do anything well if your mood and mode are not in sync. Turn your thoughts inward and concentrate on what needs to be done. Life can be like driving on ice. When you get into a bind and start sliding, you need to turn into the slide, not lock up your brakes. That's often easier said than done. With S.O. you need to turn *into yourself,* or you are going to be out of control. Develop a homing thought— one you can return to when you need to stay centered. How about "I'm at peace with myself and others."

• Once you get on a roll, don't stop. You could think of it like a train trying to build up steam. Once the train starts going, it's full steam ahead. Every time it stops, the engine has to build up steam again. The idea is to keep on chugging.

• Don't let someone else make important decisions

for you. If you wait too long to do something, someone else will do it instead and you're probably the loser. The result won't be what you wanted and it could drastically affect your life. Forever. If you were offered a job and waited too long to respond, that job will be given to someone else. If you were getting a divorce and your spouse took the initiative to get an attorney first and serve notice, you probably wouldn't like the outcome.

* Have a passion for whatever you want in life. Go for it.

* Remember that actions speak louder—much louder—than words. Do what needs to be done rather than to talk about it. Talking can be draining. Conversations can be boring and you start to drift and take mini-mind-vacations. Talking may relax others but not you. You get antsy. Combine weeding a garden while conversing or take a long walk while you talk to a friend.

* Don't procrastinate or piddle. Get everything you need for a project gathered ahead of time. If you're going to write a letter, get your paper, envelope, pen, stamp, and the address before you sit down and start to write. If you're going to paint a bathroom, remove the towel racks, mirror, and medicine cabinet ahead of time. Stir the paint; get the brushes, roller and roller pan, masking tape, drop cloths, ladder, and rags. Now you're ready to begin.

* Stay away from negative people who only want to argue or putdown others. Being around negativity is like being around someone with the flu. It's contagious so keep your distance. unfortunately, negativity is a sickness that has reached epidemic proportions. Negativity can be like a curve ball; be ready to jump out of the way.

* Focus or imagine a good outcome to the situation. This is better than using willpower (which can be

negative; willpower is using sheer force by saying to yourself, "I'm going to do it no matter what!") Imagination is positive and tranquil. Redirect your energy so your stomach is not tied in knots, but be determined to achieve a goal. Focus, don't force.

• Sally was tired of arguing with her husband so she chose a calming word, peace, to help her focus. She would walk into a different room and breathe deeply several times, focusing on a good outcome like a hug and a smile from her husband.

• Symbolism is a good way to redirect your thoughts. For instance, every time you see a traffic signal, think of a project you need to do or a goal for which you are striving. When the signal is green, you think of your goal. Green is for *go*. When you see a red traffic signal, think of something you want to stop doing, like giving up smoking or griping. Every time you see the red light, say, "I have stopped." When you see the yellow caution light, it may signal that you need to stop being late for work and take caution to ensure your job security. Using symbols in this way reinforces your goals on a daily basis.

When you hear an alarm clock ringing or buzzing, think of waking up to the new you and the commitment you made to accomplish one chore each day. You can use other symbols like a bank sign to indicate getting your finances in order or a billboard with your name and accomplishment written across it: Joe just graduated from welding school!

If objects don't work well for you, try certain words (for example, the word cool) or phrases. When you hear your chosen word or phrase, associate it with your new temperament. A phrase such as "start your engines" can cause a racecar driver to focus. Movie stars learn to focus instantly when the director says, "Lights, Camera, Action." As a child when you played hide and seek and you heard the final warning of "ready or not, here I come," you knew you had better be in your hiding place.

Certain days of the week can have a significant meaning as well; Monday may indicate laundry day or time to pay bills. Saturday may mean it's time to mow the grass and call distant family members to check on them. If you've set aside certain days for certain jobs, then you won't watch television or go somewhere until those chores are finished.

* Learn to rate your catastrophes from one to ten, and don't sweat the small stuff.

* Don't let your mind dwell on the reactions of the physical body. Detach yourself. You don't stop fear by denying it. You face it. Face your experience whether it's butterflies in your stomach, wobbly knees that feel like they won't hold you up, a voice that cracks or stutters, or sweaty palms. Witness your uneasiness as an out-of-the-body experience. Pretend someone else is giving the speech.

Doing something new can be fearful. It takes you out of your comfort zone. But, whether it's a job interview or a court hearing, don't turn your back on fear. It will bite you in the butt. Instead, bravely face up to your responsibility or put your new ideas into motion. Only back away from fights, never from duty. Making excuses won't change a dissatisfied life, but action will. Face it, life is disruptive. We have to stop to answer the phone, cook meals, do chores, and run errands, Find a way to deal with life and its disruptions.

COMMITMENT STIRS UP A HORNET'S NEST OF EMOTIONS

Once a commitment is made, we experience a whole gamut of emotions. First there's excitement, then comes overwhelming fear. We question why we ever did it—whatever *it* is. Despair sets in and we can't see the light at the end of the tunnel. We think how much easier it would have been if we'd just trudged along, staying with the old ways. We were more comfortable then because we at least knew where we stood. Now the unknown is ready to swallow us alive.

unfortunately, without a commitment, nothing will happen.

This is the time you need unshakeable self-confidence and faith. Write your commitment on a sticky note and post it where you won't lose sight of it. Each day take one step toward this goal, whether it's going to the library to check out books about a new career or hobby, or to buy a trade paper to locate contacts.

The strangest things will begin to happen. You may receive unsolicited mail on that subject matter, or you might meet someone, the exact person who can help you achieve your goal.

Know that something grand is going to happen to you this week. Say it out loud and believe it. This type of affirmation gives your commitment positive energy. If a negative thought creeps into your mind, don't finish the thought. Start humming a tune or spelling a word like *success*.

Having Stimulus Overload is like riding your bicycle down a steep hill and getting the high-speed wobbles. If you aren't committed to what you've begun, you'll wreck for sure. If you do manage to hold on, you're still in for a rough ride, but like every other challenge, you'll feel such relief at the end of the ride.

How do you spell relief?

• Recognize what sets you off and trips your trigger.

- Eliminate stress; engage in exercise.

- Look before you leap.

- Initiate coping plans.

- Expect obstacles (but move ahead anyway).

- Focus on your goal.

Here are several challenges that will only take ten minutes to complete. Just think; in less than half an hour, you can get three chores done.

1. Pick up the phone book and look up the number of someone you need to call.
2. Make an appointment (dentist, credit counselor, massage, lawn estimate).
3. Make out a grocery list.
4. Sort a load of laundry.
5. Throw a load of clothes into the washing machine.
6. Clean out the glove compartment of your car.
7. Clean out one dresser drawer.
8. Look in your closet and find one thing that no longer fits you. Give it away.
9. Sew on a button.
10. Cut your toenails.
11. Throw away junk mail.
12. Sweep the kitchen floor.
13. 1 3. Empty trash cans.
14. 1 4. Clean off one shelf in the refrigerator.
15. 1 5. Polish a pair of shoes.
16. Stop by the bakery on the way to work to buy a dozen cookies for your co-workers.
17. Stop on your way home from work and buy a "thinking of you" card to send to a friend or loved one.
18. Mark your calendar for important things to do this

week.

19. Pay a bill.
20. Cancel a subscription for a magazine you no longer
    have time to read.

WORDS OF WISDOM

You cannot escape the responsibility of tomorrow by evading it today.

—Abraham Lincoln

Many of life's failures are people who did not realize how close they were to success when they gave up.

—Thomas Edison

The great thing in this world is not so much where we are, but in what direction we are moving.

—Oliver Wendell Holmes

The road to hell is paved with good intentions.

—Jerry Augustine

I know God will not give me anything I can't handle.

I just wish that he didn't trust me so much.

—Mother Teresa

I have learned that success is to be measured not so much by the position that one has reached in life as by the obstacles which he has overcome while trying to succeed.

—Booker T. Washington

Worry and anxiety are sand in the machinery of life; faith is the oil.

—E. Stanley Jones

. . . If at first you don't succeed, try, try, try again.

—W.E. Hickson

Nothing in the world can take the place of persistence.

Talent will not;

Nothing is more common than unsuccessful men with talent.

Genius will not;

Unrewarded genius is almost a proverb.

Education alone will not;

The world is full of educated derelicts.

Persistence and determination alone are omnipotent.

—Calvin Coolidge

That which does not kill me makes me stronger.

—Nietzche

QUESTIONS TO ASK YOURSELF

Learn more about yourself by answering the following questions. In the parenthesis are some examples. Write your answers right in the book. Be honest with yourself.

1. What makes you angry? (instructions that aren't clear, manipulators, rude people)
2. What happened the last time you lost your temper?
3. How could you have prevented it?
4. Which topic of discussion stresses you the most? (in-laws, money matters, sex, kids)
5. What are your actions when you are impatient? (pace, interrupt, complain, get abrupt)
6. How can you change? (count to ten, ask to speak to a supervisor, take deep breaths)
7. What behavior do you most want to change? (anger)
8. 52 JORJAN JANE
9. How can you change that behavior? (think of the personas your grandmother)
10. What scares you? (being alone, getting a divorce, losing a job, a burglar in your home)

11. Who do you need to forgive? (neighbor, co-worker, family
12. member)
13. On a scale from one to ten (with ten being the highest), rate your physical health.
14. On a scale from one to ten, rate your emotional health.
15. On a scale from one to ten, rate your spirituality.
16. Where can you walk or drive that has a peaceful environment?15. What are your best physical traits? (height, eyes, hair, butt)
17. What are your best character traits? (honesty, optimism, fairness, dependability)
18. What are your worst traits? (impatience, jealousy, temper, dishonesty)
19. What do you do to help you focus? (breathe deeply, find a quiet place)
20. When do you hyper focus? (when you hear an intruder in the house, when there is an emergency)
21. What impulse do you need to control? (interrupting, rage, yelling, hysteria)
22. How do you plan to do it? (imagine a good outcome, focus on a word or phrase)
23. How are you going to get over the loss of a good friend?
24. (socialize more, join a group)
25. What can you do to be more organized? (pay bills on
26. Monday, write out a daily list of things to do)
27. Are you a giver or a taker?
28. Are you a consumer or a producer?
29. Name something you did for which you are proud.
30. What drives you crazy? (fingernails scratching on a blackboard, someone tapping a pen, irresponsible cell phone usage)
31. What do you do when you realize you need help? (nothing—just pout, call a hotline, phone a friend, see a

minister, talk to a therapist)

32. What are you afraid to admit to anyone? (that you don't do your job well, that you are afraid to be alone)

33. What is missing in your life? (romance, a good income, fun) 31. How do you get ideas? (reading magazines, watching commercials, driving in the mountains)

34. How often are you sick?

35. What happened the day before you got sick? (argued with spouse, were rejected for job promotion)

36. 34. Is there any connection between the event and your illness? 35. When was the last time you borrowed something from someone?

37. Did you return it in the same condition?

38. What is the most money you ever lost gambling?

39. How much money have you lost gambling in the last ten years?

40. When was the last time you were hungry but had no money to buy food?

41. How much money do you have left to save after payday?

42. What sparks your interests? (a magazine article, a movie, a seminar, watching television)

43. Rate your job performance (on a scale from one to ten with ten being the highest).

44. Rate your confidence level (jobwise) on a scale from one to ten.

45. Rate your self-esteem (on a scale from one to ten).

46. Rate yourself as a spouse (on a scale from one to ten).

47. Rate yourself as a parent (on a scale from one to ten).

48. Have you ever done the same things as a parent that you said you wouldn't do when you became one? What things?

49. When were you lost?

50. When was the last time you cried? Over what?

51. What grates on your nerves? (barking dog, women who

baby-talk)

52. What makes you feel guilty?
53. What positive thing do you do to find relief? (jog, dance, sing)
54. What negative thing do you do to find relief? (drink, gamble, take drugs)
55. How do you think other people see you? (moody, intelligent, honest, antsy)
56. Name one important thing you need to do. Do it tomorrow.
57. What makes you sad?
58. What would make life easier for you? (housekeeper, decent car, better job)
59. Where can you go to find a quiet spot?
60. What has a friend done to hurt your feelings? (betrayed loyalty, tried to get your job)
61. As a child what were you best at doing? (climbing trees, showing off, dancing)
62. As a teenager what were you best at doing? (skateboarding, playing guitar, rapping)
63. As an adult what were you or are you best at doing?
64. (writing poetry, cooking, woodworking)
65. I suggest that you come back to this chapter from time to time. Look over your answers. Add new thoughts or ideas. Doing this will give you some insight about who you are and how you think.
66. Do you see a pattern of behavior? Can you see what you need to change or how much you have already changed?

CHAPTER 5

THINGS THAT WE NEED TO OVERCOME

Clutter drives us crazy, yet we're surrounded by it. We can't throw anything away, but if we had someone who really needed the items we might discard, it would make sorting through the stuff much easier. We'll always have more than we need because we stockpile.

My friend Barbara shares her story. "I have always been thrifty and look for bargains, but I am obsessed with shopping. I will buy anything that is on sale whether I need it or not. I justified my purchases by saying that I need these things for a rainy day. Sometimes I will buy an item as a gift, but the gift usually stays with me.

"I have a pantry filled to the ceiling. My clothes cupboard is so full that I have difficulty getting to an outfit that I want to wear. I finally got fed up with all the mess and literally cleaned house. Now when I get the urge to go shopping, I don't because I think of all the rabbit trails I had in the house: the magazines and newspapers that I hadn't read, all piled high along the living room wall, the boxes of fabric that I was going to use, someday. There were the two extra sets of dishes that I had sitting out on my kitchen cabinet along with a wok, which I never used, and a coffee grinder that I used once. I had saved every paper bag from the grocery store for the past ten years and I had a sack full of little wire bread ties.

"At last, I can invite someone over without having to remove last year's tax receipts from a chair in order for them to sit. I can sit at the kitchen table without having to shove all the mail to one side just to place a coffee cup. I feel so unencumbered and wish it hadn't taken me so long to clean the clutter."

Impatience is another of our problems. It's the desire for a quick fix. Addicts are obsessed with quick fixes, one right after the other. Impatient people change cars, jobs, spouses, and apartments frequently.

Start doing whatever you can to curb those small annoyances like waiting in a long line at the store or bank. Don't go on Friday, after work, when everyone else is there cashing their paychecks. If you're in a traffic tie-up, sing along with the radio. Think of something funny that you saw in a comedy. Draw a "happy face" on your dusty dashboard, make out a grocery list, or wave to a child in a passing car. Impatience leads to anger, and . . .

Anger is our worst trait, and most difficult to get under control. It is like the fog distorting the way. You need to ask yourself if another person caused your anger or if it's something internal. If you feel like the King of the Mountain and are empowered by anger, then seek professional help.

It's important to divert hostilities and have a tight rein on your emotions. Otherwise, there will be an adverse effect on you— physically, spiritually, and mentally. The physical effects include high blood pressure, heart attacks, and strokes. You can first see the signs when your breathing starts to change, becoming more rapid. Your heartbeat increases, your pulse rate rises, your muscles tense, and you may even begin to sweat. There's definitely something happening inside your body.

Emotions sneak up on you and take over. It's okay to get angry— I know I do—but it's not okay to hurl your fury onto someone else. You can scream into a pillow or punch the sofa until you're exhausted. You can go into the restroom at work or school and make a fist, curl your toes, tense your body tightly, and then let go and feel the release. Do it again and again until you're calm. Most of the time you are mad at yourself for something —for forgetting an important date or losing paperwork. Unfortunately, you are your own worst enemy.

Mentally, anger is too disruptive, because when you're angry, you block everything else out. The only thing you can feel is the rage, and like the bull seeing red, you charge. You may be replaying old tapes from the past, uprooting old hurts and transgressions.

Spiritually, when you lose your temper, you don't feel worthy. You have an obligation to yourself—and to others—to do the right thing.

An avid sports fan says, "Going to basketball games used to be my favorite pastime until I found myself getting madder and madder over a bad call by a referee or an obnoxious fan from the opposing team. I shoved someone down in his seat because he was standing and blocking my view.

If my team lost, I was devastated. I would get in confrontations in the parking lot when someone made a snide remark about my team. Now I watch the games on TV and avoid the anger."

Confusion is another problem for those of us with Stimulus Overload. You get confused because you try to bypass the reading of the instruction book. Then you get frustrated because you don't understand. When you get that blank look on your face, it's time to start all over again, this time with the manual close at hand.

Does this sound familiar?

"I got so frustrated when I tried to put some cardboard file boxes together. There were only four steps. I had read each step about ten times, and it still didn't make any sense. I got in the car and drove to the office supply store to get help. I was at my wits end. 'Why can't I fold these boxes,' I blurted to the salesman? 'I must be brain-dead. I can't figure out steps b, c, d.' He laughed as he easily assembled one right before my eyes. He made it look so simple. Why couldn't I figure that out, I thought. Feeling like an ignoramus, I shook my head in disbelief and thanked him. Once I got to my car, I immediately wrote down each step so I wouldn't forget by the time I got home. Just a little chore became overwhelming. I lost so much time that I didn't get my paperwork filed and stored as planned. Maybe tomorrow?"

Distractions/Concentration also present problems for us. Does this person's story remind you of your own life?

"There is no way of ignoring outside stimuli or noise. I can be sitting in a restaurant and hear every conversation going on at once. The young couple behind me can't decide if they want walnut or oak furniture. The two couples in the corner are discussing a trip to Cabo next month. The man with false teeth, sitting across from me, is crunching his food and slurping his coffee. It is driving me crazy! The ceiling fan has a squeak, and I can't ignore its rotation going around and around. The light over the kitchen door keeps blinking and there is a buzzing sound coming from the fluorescent light overhead. A businessman wearing the most delightful smelling cologne just walked by my table. He has on an expensive navy blue suit but is wearing a clashing lime green tie that hurts my eyes when I look his direction.

"I hear everything, see everything, and feel everything—whether I want to or not. In my line of work, it has worked to my advantage. I instinctively know what is not in place by the subtlest of clues. That was a helpful trait as a police officer."

The following example will show you how the lack of concentration makes you run around like a drunken monkey but know this: if you stick with the job, you'll get it done.

"If anyone saw how I clean house they would ship me off to the funny farm. I'll start one job and then switch midway to another, then another. I will find myself changing sheets, then arranging books in the library, running off to dust in the living room, going back to make up the bed, heading back to empty a trash can, but I only get to the next room when I remember that I owe a friend a letter. I'll sit down at the desk but get only two paragraphs written when I look at the clock and realize that the mailman will be coming soon. I grab an envelope to write the address, but I can't locate it. I waste twenty minutes looking for it, then decide to update my Rolodex with new addresses. I have a stern talk with myself, because this time- consuming project doesn't fit the category of housecleaning and that happens to be my priority today.

"I realize I need to throw some clothes in the washer, but before I get to the laundry room, I stop in the kitchen to wash a few dishes. I only get the sink filled with water when I see the trashcan that I forgot to empty. I walk by the cupboard and get the vacuum out and carry it upstairs where I vacuum half of the carpet, then head to the laundry room again. I trip over the broom, so I decide to sweep the kitchen floor. Let's see now, what was I doing before sweeping. You get the picture.

"Rarely would I finish one job before flitting off to do another. Of course, I know I get distracted easily, but I have learned to live with it. I dance and sing while I'm cleaning house. I may run outside to pick flowers to fill an empty vase on the coffee table in the midst of dusting it. I may watch a little bird build a nest and make up a poem about it and not finish the dusting for another hour. A mediocre day becomes special and productive for me. If I set a time limit of five hours to clean house, and I have wasted the first two hours without one job completed, that's okay. I know that I now need to kick into a higher gear. I also know that I can't prioritize jobs so I allow one hour to just get started in the right direction.

"Getting started is tough for me. It gets worse before it gets better, but I will finish in the allotted time if I don't answer the phone or visit with someone. Sure, it will have been done piecemeal, but nevertheless it is all done."

I can easily lose track of what I'm doing when distracted, yet on the flip side I can be fast, focused, and efficient, doing fives things at once. It's like watching a video on fast forward. The only thing consistent with me is inconsistency. Are you the same way?

Forgetfulness. Get in the habit of always placing your car keys in the same place. Do the same with your wallet and glasses, otherwise you'll waste too much time looking for them. It's also wise to have an extra car key and house key to keep in your wallet.

When your routine changes and you're stressed, you will be more forgetful. So remind yourself that you have something important to do. Change your watch to the other wrist, put a bandage on your finger, paint a dot of correction fluid on your index finger, put a colorful ponytail tie around your wrist, or wear a reflective bicycle band around your arm.

Sadly, there are parents with S.O. who will forget anything that is not engrained in a schedule. They will put their child in the back seat of their car and head to work. After an eight-hour shift they return to the car and realize they forgot to drop the child off at the babysitter's. This occurs every summer in Las Vegas where our summer temperatures soar, making the temperature inside the car hit one hundred sixty degrees or more. Tragically children die every year from a parent's forgetfulness. Of course, it wasn't intentional but imagine how devastated you would be— and how angry at yourself.

Don't let something like this happen to you. Take drastic measures to prevent it. Take your kitchen timer along and set it to go off at the approximate time you'd arrive at the sitter's house or put an emergency flasher on the front seat of your car. Tie a scarf around your steering wheel to remind you that something is different today. Do whatever it takes to remember.

On a more positive note, there is an advantage to forgetfulness. That advantage occurs during distraction or diversion when we completely forget about being broke, hungry, or irritated. Movies work wonders to give us a temporary reprieve.

Has this happened to you?

"I told a friend that I would pick her up for work since her car was in the repair shop. I never gave it another thought until I got to work and the boss asked if any of us had heard from Judy. Oh Damn!" **Sensitivity** to smells can cause a physical reaction.

"I am extremely sensitive to smells. There are some places that I never want to return such as New Orleans in the summer with its stuffy, musty, mildewed smell, or just outside of Dodge City, Kansas where there are miles of cattle feeding lots and stockyards. Mobile, Alabama is another place that I don't want to be when the wind is blowing and I am down wind of the paper factory. Other places that get me down are the fish stand at Seattle's Pikes Place Market and the wharf in San Francisco. I could go on and on, but you get the point.

«I don't like the smell of fish, farm animals, dairies, tire shops, fiberglass repair shops, roofing tar, tanneries, rotten potatoes, baby diapers, dog manure, garbage dumps, or the smell of stale beer and smoke in a bar. My mom used to think that I was just being dramatic when I gagged and vomited. She wanted me to quit acting like the smell was going to kill me. I couldn't. I didn't want to be affected so profoundly by these odors, but they were terrible—unbearable.

«As a cop, I used to carry a small jar of vicks to use in my nose if I went on a homicide. Otherwise, the stench would stay in the hair of my nose for days. On the other hand, I get great enjoyment from the fragrance of certain perfumes, flowers and spring rain, pizza parlors, pies baking, barbeque on the grill, and Thanksgiving dinner.»

Another example of a problem with sensitivity—this time, emotional sensitivity—is crying at sad movies, watching someone say goodbye at the bus station, or being overly sensitive to remarks about weight, appearance, or a disability.

Rejection and criticism can be hard to handle calmly. A friend told me that in order to avoid crying when her boss is chewing her out, she pretends he's really yelling at a co-worker. This allows her to stay calm until she gets home where she can sort it all out. She said that even if he's giving her constructive criticism, she's prone to getting upset.

"Once I cried at a parent/teacher conference when the teacher told me that my son was not a good student and had a discipline problem. It was as though she was telling me I was a bad mom. I was hurt and insulted."

Sequence is another big problem for someone with Stimulus Overload.

"I always get the cart before the horse. I will purchase a scarf, then shop for a week to find an outfit to match. When I'm cooking, I don't coordinate the length of time for each item. The vegetables will be done, but the meat is still rare. The rolls will be burnt and the salad not made yet.

"I'll pay bills before adding a deposit in the checkbook so I end up with a minus balance and have to cross out and begin again. I'll make a list of errands to run, but on the way I change my mind. Instead of going to the bank where I was headed first, I turn around and go to the grocery store and drug store and never get to the bank that day." **Blame and denial** are two ugly traits.

The quickest way to spot immaturity is to watch those who constantly blame others for their problems in life. If, for example, I offered to drive my neighbor to the store and I then had a wreck, it's not her fault. Yet I might say, if she hadn't imposed on me, I wouldn't have been in this situation. Once you make the commitment, anything that follows is your responsibility. This is worth repeating: Once you make the commitment, anything that follows is *your* responsibility. If you don't want to do something, say so ahead of time, but don't blame someone else for your accidents.

Bill, age fifty-three, a divorced, unemployed alcoholic says, 'For years I was in denial. When I was thrown in jail again for DUI, I told myself that it wasn't my drinking, but the overzealous cop trying to make his quota. I can stop drinking anytime I want. I'm in this treatment center because my attorney said that the judge would go easy on me if I agreed to treatment.

When my wife left me, I said good riddance. She was a control freak anyway. It had nothing to do with me. When I was fired from my job, I told myself that I had a boss from hell, never admitting that I was unreliable, calling in sick from hangovers and being tardy too many times. Everyone in my life was too demanding—my wife, my boss, the cop, the judge, the doctor, and the neighbors. I found fault with everyone, even my kids who preferred to stay away because all I did was argue and rationalize.

"My personality changed from jovial to mean and nasty. I blamed everyone except myself. The third DUI and another stint in a treatment center finally brought me to realization. I cried over all my missed opportunities with my wife and kids, but tomorrow will be different. I will take one day at a time and rebuild my self- esteem."

Despair can overwhelm. Stay busy: volunteer, join a club, go to church, meet others for lunch, make new friends, serve lunch at a food kitchen. Then count your blessings. All of these are good diversions.

Frank, age seventy, lost his wife a year ago and fell into a deep state of depression. He says, "I had never paid bills, cooked, or cleaned. My daughter helped for a while, but she had her own life to live. I was overwhelmed and it threw me into a tailspin. I thought that I was suffering from Alzheimer's, but the doctor said that I wasn't. I finally went to a support group, because I didn't know where else to go. My life turned around. I met interesting people who encouraged me to volunteer at the hospital on weekends, which I did. My grandson told me that his school needed a crossing guard, so off I went for an hour each morning. I started going to church again. I never thought that I could survive after losing a loved one, but we are stronger than we think. Recapture your spirit."

Worry is another trait we need to curb. Mike, a construction supervisor, age forty-four, divorced with custody of his nine-year- old daughter, tells his story. "I have a fear of not being in control. I worry all the time. I come across as being self-assured, but I don't know what the future holds in store for me. I don't want anyone to know how insecure I feel. The question is always lurking: What if . . . What if I lose my job? What if I get sick? What if I wreck my truck? What if the new plans for the freeway come through the middle of my house? What if I can't pay my bills? What if my new girlfriend breaks up with me?

"The worry never seems to end. I'm so afraid of making the wrong move that sometimes I do nothing. I keep thinking that my ex-wife will go back to court to get custody of Dina. When she has Dina for the weekend and doesn't bring her back on time, I worry that she left the state with her."

Accept the fact that in everyone's lifetime the following things are going to happen. Be prepared to deal with them when they do occur.

Everyone will

Get blamed for something they didn't do Lose their keys (so be prepared and have extra sets made ahead of time)

Lock their car keys in the car (have a spare in your wallet) Will be in a wreck

Will lose their wallet, purse, or credit cards Will lose a loved one

Will open mouth and insert foot (probably many times)
Be in love

Get their heart broken

Have a case of mistaken identity

Break something that belongs to someone else

Get lost

Trip and fall

Go to the hospital

Be a witness to a wreck or a fight

Be confused about insurance

Forget to pay a bill, send in a form on time, etc.

You are not alone. Repeat this out loud: You are not alone.

CHAPTER 6

MARRIAGE AND RELATIONSHIPS

It is important to have your priorities straight. Someone to love and to be loved in return are at the top of the list along with food, shelter, clothing, and a job. Good relationships can lower your stress hormones, help preserve your cognitive thinking, and prevent depression.

Since we all have things we dislike doing, it's wonderful to have a spouse or friend who is good at those very things—and vice versa. Hopefully your various skills and experiences will complement each other. Problems can arise if you're just like your partner because now there are certain jobs neither of you want to do, like paying the bills or taking the car in for repairs. Then it's a coin toss to see who gets stuck with the job.

No one ever likes one hundred percent of his or her duties, at home or at work, but if you can live with eighty percent satisfaction, that's good. It also helps if the person you're living with has organizational skills to keep you on the right path, but don't mistake that person's helpful suggestions as nagging or criticism.

There are some chores your partner can't help you with. No one is able to clean off your desk, organize your bills, or handle your correspondence. Only you know where to find things. It may not look like it, but there is a method to your madness and continuity to the clutter. The pile of scrap paper on the left side of your desk may indicate the "to do" lists you made on Tuesday. The stack of envelopes on the right may be bills already paid. The advertisements piled on the floor are the ones you need to browse through and the brochures next to the lamp are to be filed. Then, of course, there's the junk mail stacked in the middle of the desk. It's been there for three weeks just waiting for you to find the time to wade through it. A mess like this could be very irritating to a tidy and orderly spouse.

A friend confessed that there was not a lot of conversation between his wife and him. She complained that his conversations were hard to follow because he switches from one thought to another without a warning or hint of transition. Jake tells his story. "That's true. I'm not a good listener, because after a few minutes my mind begins to drift. Since I'm impatient, I start fidgeting. I wish that my wife would just get to the point. Doesn't she realize that I have other things to do? She emphasizes that I am rough around the edges and won't sugar coat anything. She said that tact is a word that I need to learn, not to be mistaken for tacky (although I can be that, too)."

Tact is important in relationships, whether it's a marriage or a friendship. Webster's Dictionary describes tact as "a skill in dealing with delicate or difficult situations, a keen sense of what to say without giving offense." To say that someone is getting lazy or fat isn't using much tact.

Tact is particularly important when dealing with appearance issues. No one is totally pleased with his or her body so if you are overweight or too thin, you aren't alone. Many movie stars are unhappy with their body images too. Don't have the poor taste to ridicule someone for something that they are very much aware of. Knowing that you have a weight problem is frustrating enough. Insults don't help, but encouragement does.

Having low self-esteem or a lack of self-confidence is hard on your relationship. If you don't know who *you* are, you can't be comfortable at home, at work, or in a social setting. In the real world, getting along with others and being sociable is more important than being educated.

Pursuing an education while in a relationship brings its own set of problems. If you are attending night school or college, you probably don't sleep enough unless you are trying to escape reality, and then you may sleep too much. Your partner will find that sleeping with you is difficult because you toss and turn constantly.

You push hard to get things done, such as repairing your car or completing an assignment, but everything always takes so much longer than planned. This leaves you feeling as though no progress is being made.

In addition, you probably don't eat right or eat regularly. Yet, if you are stressed, you may overeat or drink too much because the word *moderation* is not in your vocabulary.

Other problems that interfere in relationships may be caused by unequal workloads, neglect of your partner, and a lack of time spent with each other.

If you are the husband, you may be spending too much time in front of the television or computer, working on your car, or drinking alone or with your buddies at the local pub. You may be relying on your wife to run all the errands, to entertain your friends, and do all the cooking, cleaning, and bill paying. And just when she thinks you are going to take her out on the town, you go to the ballgame with your buddies instead. It's your nature to bring home strays like the friend who lost his job or your high school buddy who is going through a divorce. No wonder your wife feels neglected.

Jake, you met him earlier, says that if his wife didn't put away his laundry after washing and folding it, it would just sit there on the dresser for weeks. He's not alone. Unless you attended a military school, you probably don't hang up your clothes either. Instead, you pile them high onto a chair until there is an avalanche. Sound familiar?

If you are the wife, you may be spending too much time with the kids, too much time at the mall, too much time on the phone, or too many hours watching television. Your husband has put in a long day at work. He comes home and has to fix your flat tire and cut the grass. You reward him by running out to a fast-food restaurant to grab something for dinner so he can clog his arteries with plaque and become a candidate for cardiac bypass surgery. Then, dinner over, you're off to a baby shower with your girlfriends.

Since you don't spend enough time with your spouse as it is, this type of behavior doesn't set well. If your car goes without oil, it won't function properly. If your flowers don't get watered, they wither and die. (Maybe all they get is a lot of fertilizer!) Yet your relationship may be one with high maintenance needs, and it still goes too long without care or attention. Is your relationship ready for a service overhaul?

Special occasions present special problems. When birthdays and anniversaries roll around, you often have no gift because you looked so hard and long to find the perfect gift that the special day slipped by, and you bought nothing. Your loved one's feelings are hurt, and no one but you knows how much time and thought went into your futile search. Of course, if you were busy, you may have spaced the whole event. If you remember at the last minute, however, don't despair. You can always go out to dinner together so it becomes a special evening for both of you.

Timing is everything in the life of someone with S.O. Your current needs become all-consuming if you have a deadline to meet (or a test or an interview). When this happens, you are mentally unavailable to meet the needs of your partner. When you have finished the IRS audit or your current work project, you will have the time to lavish your loved one with attention. You will feel like a can of cola that's been shaken. When you pop the lid, it spews and bubbles everywhere from the release of pressure.

If you are the husband, you will probably send your wife flowers or buy her a pair of earrings to match her favorite dress. You're romantic when you have the time, so pamper her. Take her to the beach to build sand castles, or to the mountains for a picnic and present her with a freshly picked bouquet of wildflowers.

If you're the wife, give your husband a well-deserved massage, and wear something sexy for him—or wear nothing at all. Don't forget his other needs like his favorite home-cooked meal, served by candlelight. Men also appreciate coming home to a clean house, even if they don't always remember to say so.

Getting away for a day or two can change your outlook and perspective. This may be the glue that holds your marriage together.

When you are broke, you can still give each other thoughtful gifts like a coupon book full of coupons to exchange for a back rub, dishes to be done, breakfast served in bed, a roll in the hay, a walk in the park—all due and payable upon presentation of the coupon. If you use your creativity, there is never a question of what to do. It's simply a matter of finding the time in which to do it and to have your mood and mode in sync.

You need to know that at the end of a hard day, your loved one is waiting for you with open arms, accepting you for what you are and vice versa. You can't worry or wonder about overspending, gambling, infidelities, or what the neighbors did. All you want is just a little peace and tranquility. You need a quiet atmosphere, not chaos, in order to unwind. If you have problems that are weighing you down, it will take your undivided attention to solve them, so hopefully your spouse or significant other will give you the space you need. You will be ever so grateful even though you rarely say so. It's times like this when a hug can be priceless.

Conflicts can cause resentment between spouses. Agree to disagree and refuse to argue over conflicting opinions that get rehashed every time you fight (whether the argument is about money issues, sex, or leniency with the kids). If there is an important issue on the table, like moving to a different town or whether to home school your kids, then set ground rules before the discussion: no back stabbing, no name calling. Schedule the discussion for a certain time such as 7:00 P.M. and then at 7:15 P.M. end the discussion and go out for ice cream. The one who keeps getting off the subject has to buy. Make it a habit to have a pleasant ending (a win-win situation) to your discussions.

It happens all too often. You tend to blow up over the slightest incident if you are stressed, and there is no consoling you. You may have to take a walk or change scenery to cool down. Until you work things out in your mind, you can't discuss the incident or be forgiving. You blame everyone else for your problems instead of taking a critical look at yourself. Needless to say, you are moody and your home life isn't the smoothest. There's a flavor of ice cream named after your relationship. Can you guess? You're right—it's "Rocky Road."

Those of us who have Stimulus Overload have to realize what the petty stuff is and not get upset over it. If your husband squeezes the new tube of toothpaste in the middle, it's not a big deal. If anything make a joke about it, but don't do it in a criticizing manner.

If you have children, you probably feel you're being pulled like taffy. Each child needs something different.

Private time between you and your spouse is likely a luxury. You try to make time for lovemaking, but the distractions are many. The children are arguing, the phone is ringing, someone is knocking on the door, or the faucet is dripping in the bathroom.

And through all of this, you're trying to focus. You feel like the Kodak advertisement, wanting to "capture the moment," but spontaneity has become a thing of the past. Understand that and put in a video for the kids. Pop some popcorn. Slumber parties can be fun for the kids but have them take turns with their friends. Their friends' parents need some quiet time too.

Despite all this, you can be ever so charming if you are not pushed for time, and if the noise level is low. Music is always a nice mood enhancer, as is the smell of soap and shampoo after a shower.

You'd like to stop jumping so many hurdles. You'd love to slow down and know the meaning of contentment, but that involves replacing old unworkable habits with new ones. Are you up to the challenge?

You have a responsibility to yourself and your loved ones to manage your time better, to live more productively, and to replace anger with exercise (even if it's just running in place).

If your relationship is turbulent, you may flounder helplessly in an effort to deal with the problems. The torment may be tearing you apart inside, yet your tendency to procrastinate is keeping you on the treadmill, running and running, getting increasingly more tired, and going nowhere. You may be anxious and wonder if you're doing the right thing.

If the previous paragraph describes you, then call a friend, a minister, or a relative. Ask them to help with ideas to resolve your problem. Any suggestions would be appreciated because it's likely you ran out of them a long time ago.

One thing you can do is to decide to be happy for one week. Both of you must agree not to argue, ridicule, or hurt the other. If that works, then prolong it for another week. To say that you are going to stick it out forever is simply too overwhelming. It's like making up your mind to quit smoking. You know that you should, but you keep putting it off. So don't say that you are going to quit forever, say that you are going to quit for a day, then for a week. Take it a little at a time so it doesn't seem impossible or drive you crazy.

Abusive relationships are all too common. When you're frustrated, you can become abusive. If you can't control your anger, it's time to see a doctor for medication. This is not something to put off. Make the phone call today. Sure, if you hit your spouse, you're sorry afterward, but that never makes it right, and it should never happen again.

How do you think your spouse feels? Abuse certainly doesn't make anyone feel loved. If your partner leaves you, it's because it's the right thing to do—for him or her. You can't worry on a daily basis whether your spouse is going to have a bad day and come home and take it out on you. What do you think that does to your spouse's self-esteem?

Everyone has bad days, and your spouse might also have Stimulus Overload and the pain and frustration that travel along with it. It doesn't matter how much you love each other; the situation can't go on. One of you must leave.

Sometimes you need to get out of a bad relationship as quickly as possible. Divorce is so crushing to your self-esteem, but you must salvage what is left and go on from there. Keep in mind that it is better to have loved and lost than never to have loved at all. Think back before you met and remember that you got along fine before you knew each other.

You may find it difficult to accept, but happiness comes from within you, not from another person. You'll be hurting all your life if you depend on other people to make you happy. Enjoy their company but learn to enjoy your own company as well.

Some type of fear or failure precedes all success. No one makes changes in life without trial and error. Success is not what you go after and achieve, but instead it's the path you take along the way to get there. It's the lessons you learn during this journey that are important—much more important than the destination.

Good relationships and strong marriages are based on love, honesty, sensitivity, trust, respect, patience, and laughter.

WORDS OF WISDOM

Do not look back in anger or forward in fear but around in awareness.

—James Thurber

This above all: to thine own self be true.

—William Shakespeare

MARRIAGE

I've never seen a perfect marriage because I've never seen a perfect person.

As humans, we all have our faults and frailties.

A good marriage requires teamwork, not competition.

It's heading in the same direction toward worthwhile goals, always striving to reach your dreams.

Marriage is a lifetime project, where selfishness is a thing of the past.

It's a leap of faith where you can hopefully land on both feet. It's being loveable when the other is being obstinate, having mutual respect for each other whether you agree or not, and never letting in-laws or kids dictate your actions. It's never swearing or throwing insults at the other, or resorting to deception or manipulation.

It's being kind in the face of rudeness, and never saying 'I told you so' or trying to get in the last word.

It's being patient when the other isn't, and a willingness to go the extra mile.

It's being compassionate when your partner is hurting, and fixing a bowl of soup when the other is sick. It's gaining an earned trust between the two of you, by always being honest, loyal and fair.

It's sharing joys, fears, a bed, and kids, and not necessarily in that order.

It's helping with the chores and the financial burden, giving no mandates or ultimatums.

There's no possessiveness because love only wants the best for the other.

It's giving a compliment when due and a wink when unexpected,

throwing in an occasional surprise and a candlelight dinner. It's forgiving and overlooking mistakes, and being as flexible as possible.

It's laughing at yourself and with each other as often as you can, and holding hands every chance you get.

It's bringing smiles to the breakfast table and sharing after-work hugs.

For the world would be a dreary place without the sunshine that you bring to each other, and the rewards of this teamwork are priceless.

It brings strength, contentment, and stability to the institution called marriage, and if it doesn't, there's no marriage, only the institution.

—G.J. Lee

QUESTIONS TO ASK YOURSELF

1. Are you a giver or a taker?
2. When are you most lovable?
3. Why did you choose your mate?
4. What do you love most about yourself?
5. What do you love most about your partner?
6. What's missing in your marriage or relationship?
7. Do you and your spouse share an equal workload at home?
8. What's the biggest mistake you ever made in your relationship?
9. When did you feel your sexiest? Why?
10. What was the biggest gamble you ever took in regard to your marriage?
11. Who loves you most?
12. Who do you love most?
13. What can you do to right a wrong in your relationship?
14. What does your partner do that grates on your nerves?
15. What do you do that irritates your partner?
16. Who decides which television programs to watch or which movie to rent?
17. What's your idea of a perfect day together, from morning to night?
18. What was the wildest thing the two of you ever did?

19. What was the nicest thing your partner ever did for you?
20. Rate your marriage on a scale from one to ten (with ten being the highest).
21. Name one important thing that you need to tell your spouse other than I love you.
22. If you only had ten minutes left to live, what would you tell your partner?
23. What one thing could your partner do to help you out?
24. What can you do to improve your marriage or relationship? Make a list.
25. What action can you take today to change your relationship?
26. Finish this sentence: You make me feel loved when . . . (then tell your spouse).
27. What were the two worst arguments you had with your spouse?
28. What needed to happen to change the outcome of the ruckus?
29. Can you admit to yourself when you are wrong? (Can your partner?)

NOTES:

CHAPTER 7

PARENTING AND THE TEENAGER

Now that you know what Stimulus Overload is all about, you'll be able to see some of the traits in your children that you see in yourself. The main thing to remember is that each child is unique and needs love and praise. How they accept it will vary. Often children shun what they need the most. Invest in your child's emotional security rather than investing in toys and games.

Children need to learn behavior management just as they learned bladder control as infants. Wetting the bed was uncomfortable and embarrassing. Everything has a consequence.

As your children grow older, teach them to be polite, not to be crude or rude. They need to learn not to interrupt while others are talking (they fear, as all of us with S.O. do, that they'll forget what they wanted to say if they wait). Set a time for them to do their homework and to go to bed. They need a schedule to follow.

When your children become teenagers, don't buy them a car. Have them get a job so they can buy their own vehicle. This helps your child learn responsibility. With any young driver, it can be dangerous to allow friends in the car, but a child with S.O. has even more problems with distraction and excitability from the conversation and radio. It's sad but necessary to mention the importance of having good car insurance that includes an accidental death and dismemberment policy. This type of insurance is called ADD—how ironic!

Most of the time a teenager doesn't have the capacity for reasoning. His brain is not fully developed. He knows right from wrong—for the most part—but so does a six-year-old. Teenagers don't look ahead to the consequences of their actions. They can't always comprehend the ramifications of being caught stealing, speeding, drinking, taking drugs, or having unprotected sex. For a moment, in the back of his mind, he has a nagging feeling that he shouldn't be doing what he's doing, but that's where his thinking stops.

Then, throwing caution to the wind and ignoring any glimmer of insight, he says, "Why not?" This has nothing to do with intelligence. Your teen might be a straight A student, but still not see the big picture. What he does see is the present. He doesn't know how to fast forward to the end or aftermath of what could be destructive behavior.

Many a teenage girl will attest to the fact that she never dreamed she would become pregnant after one careless moment in the back seat of her boyfriend's car. Nor would the young fellow who took his friends on a joy ride, in his parents' car without permission, ever believe he'd be involved in a wreck, maiming or killing his passengers.

Teenagers need to feel useful and needed. They need to feel they are a part of the family. Ask your teen to repair something for you, to fix a flat tire, to wash the car or cut the grass, or even to paint a room in your house.

Kids need the experience of doing something well so they are left with a sense of accomplishment. This builds confidence. They need to know, deep inside, that they're good at something. Not just because someone told them so, but also because they intuitively feel it. Sometimes just knowing a job was well done is the only reward necessary.

Teaching your children manners and discipline is also important, but this is best taught through setting a good example. I dislike the expression, "Do as I say, not as I do." What kind of message do you send your children when you use that statement? Is it, "I'm an adult and I can do what I damn well please"?

Some kids never get over the damage done by a controlling parent. If you're a teenager reading this book, strive to be the best you can be—at whatever you do. If a parent belittles you, a friend betrays you, a boss threatens you, or a girl/boyfriend dumps you, remember this: the only thing keeping you afloat is your self-worth.

Have a conversation with yourself. Weigh the facts. Change if needed, but *know* that you are okay with or without anyone else's approval.

The teenager with low self-esteem is the one who feels rage when he's bullied or teased at school or on the street corner. He may even be driven to the edge, pushed to the point where he goes on a rampage and kills others.

It's like a child having a temper tantrum, so filled with fury and anger, saying, "I'll show you. I'll get your attention." In his immature mind, he feels this proves to the world that he really is somebody, that he exists and doesn't have to take any ribbing or abuse ever again.

The rage grows, like the devil's poking him in the rear, pushing him closer and closer to the point where he can't stop. A teen filled with rage may even make it worse by holding it in long enough to plan an elaborate scheme that brings harm to many other innocent people. We've all seen news reports of school shootings. What terrible tragedies these are, to the family, the victims and their families, the police, and the community.

The teen never stops to realize that his parents or family may never be able to live in that same town again. They will be sued and will shoulder the expenses of court costs, funeral expenses, and more.

There's the trauma to the victim's parents and family, the hatred they feel, and the gnawing inside them because they need to forgive but can't. There's the anguish of the police officer—and many sleepless nights— because he had to shoot the teenager—a child— who wouldn't drop the gun. There's a scar on the community that won't go away.

Like a child who commits suicide, this teen is asking for help in the only way he or she knows how. It's the ultimate cry for attention, for someone to take over and help him get what he needs. He needs to feel worthwhile and loved for his good attributes before everything goes awry, or before he becomes despondent.

At times it's impossible for your children to buckle down and do what is necessary. What a struggle they have. They may be dealing with raging hormones, acne, identity crisis, and the need to show some independence. A teenager gets angry, withdraws, becomes remorseful, and then begins the cycle all over again. A parent can't yell and scream because this tactic does not work. Neither does grounding, particularly when the child suffers from S.O. or ADD.

Parents may think that if they're not hard enough on the child, that he may let a promising future slip away. This method just doesn't work and often takes a great toll. Kids don't hear what you're saying unless it's a compliment to them or something of extreme interest. You're talking to him. He's looking at you, but even though the lights are on, as the saying goes, no one is home.

The kid is often daydreaming or thinking of the soccer game on Saturday. He could be trying to figure out how to ask you for the car tomorrow, or cooking up a scheme to try and get a little extra cash for the weekend. What you have to say is of little importance when he's busy trying to get his way.

Keep your explanations short and sweet. He'll hear what you're saying if you keep it under one minute. Lectures don't work— they are tuned out.

Discipline is essential, but make it quick because it's more effective. No television tonight is better than no television for a month. You won't be home every day to enforce it, but you will be home tonight. And that will get your point across.

Extra-curricular activities are very important. The busier your child is, the better he will be. Look into after-school activities such as sports, music lessons, or classes in art, stained glass, car repair, cooking, or woodworking —or whatever interests your child.

If your child or teen is a delinquent, he hasn't yet learned from his mistakes. It's difficult to put together the consequences of his behavior or aggression. Certain parts of the story are simply missing and it's like jumping from page one to page four. He's missed a big and important segment and is trying to follow through without all the facts. And unfortunately it seems that some children never do learn.

As I mentioned earlier, according to some researchers, a teenager's brain isn't fully developed yet. Some also contend that the brain of those with ADD or S.O. is smaller than average but no less the smarter. There's just a different method needed to get these children where they're going.

Please, if you're a teenager, remember this: We never learned how to think things through from beginning to end because we don't understand the process of sequencing. If we don't understand every step along the way, we fall behind.

Don't be embarrassed to ask the teacher to repeat what she just said if you didn't comprehend. If you still don't get it, speak to her after class or ask one of your classmates to explain it again. If necessary, talk to your parents about arranging for a tutor for you.

Jan, age twenty, a high school dropout, drug addict, and prostitute asked if I would relay her story in the hope that it may help someone else learn how to cope (both as a teenager and a parent). "I convinced myself that I was dumb because I did so poorly in school. Dad said that I just wasn't trying hard enough. I was held back a year, but that didn't help. The truth was that I didn't know how to study and I was dyslexic. It was easier to quit than to go through all the ridicule. I turned to drugs. It made me feel smarter and less inhibited. It was my escape from reality or so I thought. I stole money from my parents to support my habit, I shoplifted, and I sold my body. I even gave up my crack-addicted baby rather than face the responsibility of raising him. Nothing else mattered except my next fix. I was in a downhill spiral. I was found in an alley with an eight-inch gash in my head, but I don't know how it happened or how I got there. I don't remember anything after being hooked on drugs.

"I only remember my first fix, and like the Energizer bunny, I just kept on going, going, going. Five years had passed, but I didn't know it. I was now twenty but looked more like forty. I weighed eighty-six pounds and my teeth were rotten. If I hadn't been hit in the head and ended up in the hospital, I would be dead today. My parents never knew where I had been all this time after they had kicked me out. I can't blame them because I was so disruptive, but they were relieved to get the call from the hospital. They helped me a lot and paid for adult education. I not only got my high school diploma but also went on to cosmetology school and became a hairdresser. I finally got in the "learning mode" and am moving forward in the right direction."

It takes sincere interest to find out what your child likes best. Find out what type of friends he associates with by having them over for a barbeque. Get to know what they are like and learn what their interests are. This will tell you a lot about your own teenager.

Allow your child the individual freedom to follow his dreams. Encourage him. Apologize to your child for not understanding his particular problems. Ask him to help you understand what he is going through emotionally. A kid can be forgiving when he knows that you are sincere.

Let your child know that there's nothing he can do to change your love for him. Sure, you get upset with him and are sometimes disappointed by his behavior, but you never—ever—stop loving him. If you withhold love as a punishment, he cannot accept himself, and a child who has been deprived and neglected doesn't understand love, only manipulation.

A child does his best when he wants to do so. If he wants to play soccer for the love of the sport, he'll do well and build self- confidence. But, if you make him play for your own personal reasons, there will be a clash of wills. If he decides to pursue the sport, it will be out of fear of rejection or punishment, or for the promise of a reward.

There will be conflicts of will that arise in every family, for many different reasons: bedtime, homework, curfew, dating, body piercing, tattoos, and clothing. Plan ahead and determine how you'll deal with these conflicts and discuss them briefly.

Children learn from what they see and hear. Since we adults with S.O. have a short fuse, we don't react calmly. What really matters, however, is how we handle it afterward.

Being hard-nosed and bullheaded just doesn't cut it. No guilt trips, please. That has residual effects and can be mentally crippling.

What is needed is unconditional love as well as a gentle steering in the right direction *every* time he seems to have lost the way. Your child really *needs* to know you love him, not just by words but also by deeds.

Your high school graduate may not be ready for college. College requires a great deal of discipline to get the assignments done on time. Starting out with a full load of classes can be overwhelming and there are lots of mandatory classes that can seem boring. Advise your teen to start slowly, by taking elective classes that interest him. vocational training is another option, and learning a trade is a valuable asset.

One of my grandsons, age seventeen, had a difficult time concentrating in school. He would get distracted by screeching tires outside the school or by watching a speck of dust float down to the floor. He disliked the rough surface of his desk where someone had carved deep initials into the wood. This wasn't a discipline problem. His mind just wasn't in the classroom with his body.

My grandson said, "I don't have the ability to concentrate. I can't shut out noise or distractions. One week before school was out for the summer, I was sitting in my car, trying to fill out a work application. The form was for a bus boy position that should have already been completed. A carload of kids pulled into the parking lot next to me with their radio blaring. I kept making mistakes on the form. I'd scratch them out, and then make another. I finally tore up the application and drove off. That's one job I won't be getting. Now if I were filling out an application for lifeguard or police cadet instead of a bus boy, I would probably give it my full attention because it's a necessary step to get an exciting job."

Dale, age twenty-nine, a probation officer told me about his early years. "As a teenager I was bad. I vandalized, burglarized, and terrorized. I ran away from home numerous times and was booked as an incorrigible kid. My parents were so frustrated that they allowed me to be emancipated by the age of sixteen. That was when the real education began. I had to take full responsibility for myself and could not blame anyone else. I grew up fast. Ironically, I became a darn good probation officer (been there—done that)."

As a parent, don't overlook the fact that many teens are on drugs today. Don't mistake some of their behavior as S.O. You can always buy a drug testing kit and randomly test your teen if his behavior warrants doing so. If the test comes back positive, get your teenager into counseling to help him deal with addiction. No one can function on their own when they have a substance abuse.

WORDS OF WISDOM

Example is not the main thing in influencing others. It is the only thing.

—Albert Schweitzer

YOUR NAME

You got it from your father

It was all he had to give

So it's yours to use and cherish

For as long as you may live,

If you lose the watch he gave you,

It can always be replaced But a black mark on your name, Son, Can never be erased.

It was clean the day you took it

And a worthy name to bear

When he got it from his father, There was no dishonor there.

So make sure you guard it wisely,

After all is said and done You'll be glad the name is spotless When you give it to your son.

QUESTIONS TO ASK YOURSELF

1. What was your biggest obstacle to overcome as a kid?
2. Who was your hero?
3. Name an accomplishment as a teenager that you were proud of?
4. What did you want to grow up to be?
5. Did you ever give in to peer pressure? Why?
6. What was the biggest argument you and your parent had?
7. Were you afraid of the dark?
8. Who listened to you most? (parent, teacher, aunt, friend)
9. What did you regret doing as a kid?
10. Did you ever feel inferior to your classmates? When?
11. Did you ever feel superior to them?
12. Who was your best friend and why?
13. As a child what were you good at doing? (swimming, drawing, ice skating, spelling, dancing)
14. As a teenager, what were you good at doing? (skateboarding, water skiing, working with electronics, computer, sewing, playing basketball)
15. As an adult, what were you good at doing? (cooking, taxes, mechanics, gardening, writing poetry)

16. Name something that made you very proud of yourself? (class president, won a spelling bee, gave blood, learned/ gave CPR, cleaned a city park, won an award)
17. What were your favorite subjects in school? (science, math, woodworking)
18. What were your least favorite subjects? (History, English)4.

CHAPTER 8

JOBS

Your job should be in line with your talents, interests, and skills. A job is right up there in importance with food, shelter, clothing, and someone to love. Are these your priorities as well?

Sometimes you may have to take any job just to have food on your table and gas in your car, but that doesn't mean that you let your dreams fall along the wayside.

When you have S.O., getting to work—or anywhere else—on time seems impossible. If you're like me, you're often late. You ask yourself, "Why go at all?"

The answer is easy. You'll lose your job if you don't. It's important to be punctual so plan ahead. Lay out your clothes, keys, etc., the night before. Have a good alarm clock—or even two—if you are hard to wake. Leave ten minutes earlier than you usually do to allow for traffic jams, accidents, or road closures. This might even save you from getting a speeding ticket, and you certainly don't need that.

There are certain jobs that you will easily recognize aren't for you. If you are not a multitasker (able to do many things at one time), for example, I wouldn't suggest being an air traffic controller or an emergency dispatcher.

I know that I'd go nuts working in a noisy newsroom, trying to write a last-minute headline story while phones are ringing, people are shouting, and equipment is buzzing. I couldn't work at the New York Stock Exchange either. I would literally be a gibbering idiot by the end of the day. No, make that after the first hour. I get the jitters just thinking about it. I couldn't work the lunch hour at a fast-food restaurant either, without being stressed.

Of course, high adrenaline jobs do keep us from being bored. We like high-risk jobs such as police officer, fire fighter, racecar driver, bull rider, rescue worker, ambulance driver, fighter pilot, or a career in sports or as a sportscaster.

For those more subdued who turn their energy inward, there are the research scientists, inventors, brain surgeons, financial wizards, and members of Mensa (a group for those individuals with a high I.Q.) who like a mental challenge rather than a physical challenge.

A surgeon once told me that before operating on any patient, he needed several minutes alone to mentally prepare himself. Then he would play classical music during the surgery to transport him to a higher level of focusing.

There are other jobs that may not be suitable for you. These include jobs where you're paid on commission.

Ron, a car salesman, says, "S.O. just simply wears me out. I'm bombarded with fragmented thoughts and sometimes paranoia. I think of them as incoming scud. There is a war going on inside of me and the only way to win is to focus on the moment. I care about my job, but it's a cutthroat business. It's really too competitive for me. I'm constantly looking around to spot a return customer. Working on commission brings out the worst in people. I wasn't raised to take something away from someone else. If I showed a car to a couple and they returned the next day to purchase it, I expect my co-workers to call me over, not to take credit for the sale."

Your best bet may be to work alone if you get angry over being competitive or are distracted easily. There are many jobs where you can do this: car mechanic, consultant, maid, florist, truck driver (long haul), delivery driver, photographer, massage therapist, landscaper, artist, architect, counselor, accountant, biologist, forest ranger, pilot, seamstress, writer, tile layer, electrician, carpenter, house painter, etc.

You may want to start your own company if you are an entrepreneur with a unique idea. Your biggest problem will be following through, because you get held up with the sequence of things. You may, for example, jump into production without a business plan.

Clint, age thirty-five, an auto parts employee, relays his need to get ahead. Unfortunately, he says he can't get his ideas onto paper. "I had a great idea for a protective covering over a seat belt. I made several of them to see how much time and money it took to make them. I figured that I could make these at home, after work. My boss said that he liked the idea and would take one hundred to start and that the chain of auto stores that I work for would probably want to order as well. Instead of being happy, I panicked. That meant that I would have to hire employees. I would have to figure how many and what wages to pay. Then I realized that they couldn't work at my home so I would need a small workshop. That would mean paying for rent, utilities, insurance. I don't have any savings so I would have to get a business loan. Oh, I forgot, I need a name for my company and a business license. I would have to follow all the requirements for employees such as Worker's Compensation, unemployment benefits, and taxes. I would have to get a bookkeeper to make out payroll checks. I would have to buy a computer and get online to advertise my product.

"Maybe I'll go to the college and inquire about business or marketing students who need credit and experience for 'on the job training.' Maybe I'll ask my boss if he wants to be my partner and invest in my venture. This is mind-boggling. Maybe I'll put it off for another year."

If you're having similar problems, *The Entrepreneur's Guide to Business Basics 101,* a book by JoAnn M. Colton, is a good place to find some expert advice.

There are many movies stars and celebrities who have Stimulus Overload. They have blazed a trail for us. There are also writers, artists, sculptors, scientists, musicians, singers, and athletes—all who are very creative and talented and have risen above the crowd. (See the list of famous people in the back of this chapter.)

On the other side of the coin are the death row inmates, the murders, terrorists, arsonists, thieves, and abusers. The most common thread among these people is that they have some form of S.O. They let their temper, emotions, greediness, and brainwashing get the best of them. Some didn't want to work, so they looked for the easy way out at the expense of others.

If you have an impulsive nature and are working around others, you must do whatever is necessary to keep from reacting when they push the wrong buttons, either inadvertently or on purpose. Some co-workers will have you pegged, and they will do anything and everything to trip your trigger just as a joke and to see your reaction.

Stop before things get out of hand. If that means breaking into a chorus of "Jingle Bells" or "Jeremiah was a Bullfrog" to get your mind off of it, just do it.

You have a choice. You can be a decent, productive person. Or you can be a jackass.

You have to learn not to react when you're the brunt end of a joke. Don't react to condescending voices or disapproving looks. There are many rude and opinionated people on this earth, but you don't have to be one of them. Why let things eat at you like a cancer taking hold and leaving nothing but an empty shell?

Don't forget—you often affect others with your unsettling remarks or sarcasm. This is called engaging mouth before engaging brain. What it boils down to is tolerance. Most people accept us for what we are, so in turn we should accept them. You can let things get you down, or you can rise above the fray.

You're going to fall from time to time. We all do. Simply pick yourself up, brush yourself off, and start all over again. You'll be a better person for it.

Learn what works for you. Be a dependable and responsible person. Be one who can walk away from impending trouble.

Maybe you are not ready to reach your full potential. Maybe you need to "add to your assets" or to your learning experiences before you reach your peak (not money-wise but knowledge- wise).

Instead of thinking of all the wasted time, think of it as an *incubation period* with ideas forming but not quite ready to hatch. We all have certain speeds at which we operate; your speed may fluctuate. When you're ready, it's like seeing the checkered flag. You will go like a bat out of hell at breakneck speeds. You can make up for lost time. When you are good at something, it gives you confidence in your ability and you can excel.

People have to make commitments in their life. It's unavoidable if you want anything.

Being dissatisfied with your present position and same old routine can help initiate a change, but you shouldn't quit your job and sacrifice financial security unless your sanity and health are at stake.

On the other hand, your job could be making you sick. If you have a lot of headaches, stomach troubles like ulcers, or you find yourself overeating, overdrinking, or overdoing anything destructive, you may be suffering from job burnout. If that's the case, it's time for a change.

Quit beating yourself up for being an underachiever or a failure. All this does is lead to poor self-esteem or depression. When your desire to change becomes as desperate as your next breath of air, you'll do something about it.

Don't be disappointed if you're thirty-nine years old and still haven't reached significant success. Unless you're a professional athlete, movie star, pop singer, or computer guru, it's not likely you will reach your pinnacle early. Few successes have been made early in age and even fewer fortunes. Winston Churchill, Grandma Moses (the painter), and Abraham Lincoln all got a late start in life. They didn't see success for their efforts for many years.

Abraham Lincoln, for example, failed in business at age twenty- one. He followed that by failing in a legislative race at twenty-two. He had another business failure at twenty-four, overcame the death of his sweetheart when he was twenty-six, and then had a nervous breakdown at twenty-seven. He lost a congressional race when he was thirty-six, lost a senatorial race at forty-five, failed in his bid to become vice president at forty-seven, and lost another senatorial race at forty-nine. At age fifty-two, Lincoln was elected the President of the United States.

Success is an attitude. I've said it before, but it bears repeating: It's not what you achieve, but the paths you take along the way to get there. It's the lessons you have learned through trial and error. It's the journey that is truly important.

If you are actively striving for something, you are not defeated even when you have temporary setbacks. But if you quit, you are defeated!

Of course, the best way to handle Stimulus Overload is to become wealthy. Then you can hire others to handle the worry and aggravation for you.

WORDS OF WISDOM

To laugh often and much,

To win respect of intelligent people

And the affection of children;

To earn the appreciation of honest critics

And endure the betrayal of false friends;

To appreciate beauty,

To find the best in others, to leave the world a bit better

Whether by healthy child,

A garden patch, or a redeemed social condition;

To know even one life has breathed easier Because you have lived.

This is to have succeeded.

—Ralph Waldo Emerson

PROMINENT PEOPLE WITH S.O.,

ADD, ADHD, OR DYSLEXIA

Through biographies and autobiographies, many prominent people have indicated their problems with dyslexia, ADD, or ADHD (ADD with hyperactivity). They have been upfront and forthright about the problems they've faced. My hat is off to them for their truthfulness and for being such an inspiration to us. Some of the people listed are deceased, but nevertheless they've made a worthwhile contribution to society.

MOVIE STARS, SINGERS AND

COMEDIENNES

Jim Carrey, Robin Williams, Jay Leno (dyslexic), Whoopi Goldberg,

Cher, Tom Cruise (severely dyslexic, memorizes lines) Dustin Hoffman, John Lennon, Steve McQueen, Ozzy Osbourne, Will Smith, George C. Scott, Suzanne Somers, Sylvester Stallone, James (Jimmy) Stewart, Henry

Winkler, Stevie Wonder, Lindsay Wagner, George Burns

ATHLETES

Michael Jordan, Magic Johnson, Bruce Jenner, Jason Kidd, Nolan

Ryan, Pete Rose, Terry Bradshaw, Greg Louganis, Carl Lewis, Babe Ruth

AUTHORS

Lewis Carroll, George Bernard Shaw, Agatha Christie, Edgar Allan Poe, Leo Tolstoy (a brilliant novelist and philosopher who flunked out of college, was disorganized, and had trouble focusing, yet wrote *War and Peace,* etc.), William Butler Yeats, Henry David Thoreau, George Bernard Shaw, F. Scott Fitzgerald, Ernest Hemingway.

INVENTORS AND SCIENTISTS

Albert Einstein (four years old before he could speak; as an adult he had difficulty expressing himself in words or written language, but was great at visualizing; others called him simple-minded), Alexander Graham Bell, Benjamin Franklin, Thomas Edison (unable to read until he was twelve), Henry Ford, Orville and Wilbur Wright, Galileo, Louis Pasteur, Sir

Isaac Newton, Wernher von Braun, Nostradamus, Socrates

COMPOSERS

Beethoven, Handel, Mozart, Rachmaninov

ARTISTS AND SCULPTORS

Rodin, Vincent van Gogh, Leonardo da Vinci, Pablo Picasso, Salvador
Dali

PRESIDENTS, WORLD LEADERS AND

OTHER PROMINENT PEOPLE

George Washington, Abraham Lincoln, Woodrow Wilson (severely dyslexic), John F. Kennedy, Dwight D. Eisenhower, Nelson Rockefeller (41st Vice President, severely dyslexic), Robert Kennedy, Prince Charles, Eleanor Roosevelt, Napoleon Bonaparte, Nasser, Lewis and Clark, (explorers), Walt Disney, Charles Schwab, Jackie Stewart (a racecar driver who can't recite the alphabet and is functionally illiterate), Steven Spielberg (filmmaker), Ansel Adams (photographer), Malcolm Forbes, John D. Rockefeller, William Randolph Hearst, William Wrigley, Jr. (of the chewing gum company), Milton Hershey (of the chocolate company), Dale Carnegie, General William C. Westmoreland, Col. Gregory "Pappy" Boyington, Admiral Richard Byrd, Eddie Rickenbacker, General George Patton (couldn't read textbooks so his mother read to him until he left home to attend West Point; as a cadet he paid classmates to read to him, yet he was a creative genius in planned battle strategy)

NOTES:

CHAPTER 9

THE LAW AND SURVIVAL TECHNIQUES

When you suffer from Stimulus Overload, you take too many risks without thinking ahead to the consequences. You don't leave early enough for work because you piddled around, then made a last-minute dash to the car. You intended to fuel your car the night before but didn't, and now the needle on the gas gauge is pointing to empty. You forgot to stop by the dry cleaners to get your suit for the wedding tonight. You arrive at work in the nick of time, and your boss asks you to work two hours overtime today. The cleaners will be closed by the time you get off and you have nothing decent to wear to the wedding except that one suit. You feel obligated to work the overtime because your boss has overlooked several late arrivals, and besides you need the extra money.

You need a plan. Go to the cleaners on your lunch break, work the needed overtime, go home and get cleaned up, wrap the wedding gift still sitting on the kitchen table, grab a banana or apple to eat on the way, and hope that there will be something to eat at the reception. Sure, you know what life is like in the fast lane; it's an every day occurrence. You take more chances than you should.

You have a tendency to speed, only to slow down at stop signs, make illegal lane changes, and honk at slow pokes driving in front of you because of your impatience and temper. If you are stressed like this most of the time, you need no more hassles. Here is your wake-up call. I'm sure that you don't want to end up in jail or juvenile hall for your disregard of the law, so abide by it.

If you're a teenager, tough love doesn't work for you. If you're given an ultimatum to shape up or ship out, you have to ship out because you don't know how to shape up. It has nothing to do with whether you are good or bad. You just don't know how to take responsibility for yourself. Your brain is misfiring, and you don't understand coping techniques yet. When you're stopped by a police officer, you are angry. You feel like you were singled out because your car is sleek and red, or maybe you convince yourself that you only ran the caution light and that's no big deal.

You may rationalize your actions instead. You missed the big picture. How many times a day do you think that a cop or a judge hears the same excuses? You want to be treated differently. The officer doesn't know you as a good and decent person. You haven't proved that to him yet. You disobeyed the law and now you're belligerent. You're angry as hell, but this is not the time to wreak havoc and let your mouth run amuck or you *will* go to jail. Then you could lose your job, car, house, and family. Having S.O. is overwhelming enough. You really don't want to deal with all of these other problems. You will end up owing bail, court costs, fines, impound fees, attorney fees, back rent—the list goes on.

Every day cops deal with murders, rapists, robbers, arsonists, and carjackers. The suspects *always* say that they were framed or just a victim of circumstances, and occasionally this is true. Innocent people will get stopped and questioned because they fit the description of a robbery suspect fleeing in a car like yours. The officer's goal is to apprehend the suspect and keep him from repeating the crime, not to waste time by taking you to jail when you let your mouth override your brain.

You may not be aware that a ticket is a courtesy and that the cop could take you to jail for the same offense. They don't because there's not enough room in the jail to house everyone. You take offense for being stopped. It's embarrassing to be spread-eagle on the hood of a car while being patted down for a weapon so you get mouthy and irate. Of course, you are inconvenienced and possibly late to work, but let the officer do his job so you can be on your way. The more you argue and rebuke, the longer the process will take.

Be polite, no matter what. *Attitude* is everything! Put your anger on hold. Yes, it will be the hardest thing you ever did, but now is the time to hyper focus and be tactful. Otherwise, you will endure the negative consequences, and it may be years before you see the light at the end of the tunnel.

It's rare that anyone is polite when they get stopped and think that they are going to jail. What you don't know is that you may be the ninth person the cop had stopped, and like Rodney Dangerfield, he gets no respect. He could be having a bad day just like any other person dealing with the public, whether as a sales clerk or an airline agent. He is not only looking for the criminals, but he's dealing with his boss and with the irate public. His sergeant has been on his back for not being detailed enough in his arrest reports; he was told to lose twenty pounds before his next police physical; and he has a subpoena for court on the day his mother is having heart surgery.

His days off have been cancelled because of an impending strike, so don't think of being a smart mouth to him. He's probably suffering from S.O. too. That may be why he is in that line of work so he doesn't get bored with the ordinary type of job. Now you have met your match and the law is on his side, so straighten up and fly right. This is one fight you are not going to win.

There must be rules or people would just do as they please. Think of it as being a parent. You have rules for your child. If not, he may go on a date and come home at three o'clock in the morning, which would not be acceptable. (If your child inherited S.O. from you, he probably would stay out that late.) Nevertheless, there *must* be rules. The teenager who stole your son's bike must go through the juvenile court system, the pervert who flashed the kids on the school playground must go to jail, and the thief who snatched your sister's purse in the mall needs to be arrested.

This may be the first hour of the cop's shift, and he knows his day will go downhill from this point on. He has the agonizing duty to tell the mother of a seven-year-old boy that a drunk driver just ran over her son. He has the duty to tell the parents of a teenager that their son was joy riding and flipped his car, crushing two passengers. He sees a bank robbery go bad and the innocent father of three children shot and killed. He arrests a protestor who later returns to bomb a clinic. He gets so fed up with the bad and the dishonest—and you want to give him a rough time because he stopped you for speeding? Don't put yourself in that position in the first place. We all have to live in this big world together, and we have to be civil toward one another.

Don't be around people you do not like, and for heaven's sake, don't look for trouble. Because it's out there, everywhere, and it's not hard to find.

Take out your frustrations at the gym or by working hard, running fast, or doing jumping jacks until you're so tired that you don't have the energy to be mad.

If you don't like a law, call the legislators in the area where you live. If you don't know who they are, ask your neighbor. Tell your legislators that you think a particular law is outdated and explain why. Ask for their input and help to make it a fair proposition (such as child custody laws). This is what a democracy is all about. Don't gripe about it; do something about it.

"We the people" are the government, not a building, not a place. We, the voters, have a choice in what happens to us. There is always someone that messes it up for the rest of us. Why not be angry with that person, instead of with the government or the justice system?

Don't misdirect your anger or look for excuses to get out of jury duty. Be able to say "Guilty" if necessary. It's not the jury system that is too lenient. It's the jurors who are making the decisions.

Laws are introduced to protect others. For example, a group of dissentients may decide that no one is going to tell them that they have to wear a motorcycle helmet. In some states, wearing a helmet is required and for good reason, but they defy the law and do as they please. As an aftermath of a cycle accident, it is evident why it's so important to protect your head. If the person survives the accident, he will likely be a vegetable the rest of his life from irreversible brain damage. He probably didn't have insurance either, so you and your neighbors and the community are going to pay higher taxes (for indigent hospital costs).

You blame the government for higher taxes, but it's the people like this who cause the rising costs. Who do you think pays the high price of rescue when someone goes mountain climbing and falls off a cliff?

You are paying for the services and expense of search and rescue teams, helicopters, paramedics, etc. It's not cheap. Can you imagine the expense of the Oklahoma City bombing, the terrorists' attacks of the twin towers and the Pentagon—the clean up, the additional overtime for special investigations, the police, the firemen, paramedics, security officers—not to mention the shattered lives left in the aftermath.

It's bad enough to see the aftermath of a tragedy, but if you have ever watched the news on television, you will see the looting as well. Maybe a tornado hit your town and you lost your home. Then to add insult to injury, there on the news you will see people stealing what little you have left. How can the public blame the government when it is the people who get out of hand?

If you have ever had a problem with the law, you may have a negative attitude toward the police. But realize that they have a job to do. If there is a riot brewing, you will be able to feel the tensions growing, so get out of the area fast before things turn ugly. The police will be there to disperse the crowd so don't be defiant. You may get sprayed with tear gas or hit by a stun gun or worse. Realize that the crowd is going to break windows, turn over cars, and hit anyone in their way as well as the police who are trying to get them to leave. This is not the time or place to make a stand. It could end up like Custer's last stand.

It's hard for the officer to be rational if he is suffering from S.O. as well. He has too many directions to watch at one time. He's dodging bottles and rocks; he's tripping over people who have fallen from all the shoving and mania. He wants to go home to his family after the shift, not to the graveyard in a coffin. You need to understand that the cop is a victim as well; he is being bombarded too.

On a daily basis, he worries that some of the cuts and lacerations he received from a fight could be from a person infected with HIV. He knows he may have jeopardized his life and that of his wife's. This is an overwhelming concern.

Sure there are a few bad cops, but there are also bad mechanics, repairmen, and doctors. Their co-workers don't even like being around them and certainly have no respect for them.

To conclude, being in trouble with the law is like stepping off the curb and seeing a tractor-trailer truck coming around the corner. If you keep going, you are going to get hit. Know when to back up. Engrain in your mind the significance of stepping back because of the severe consequences that follow. Remember, when the police officer gets mad at you, you have pushed the wrong buttons. You know a lot about getting mad because it's a big part of your life. Believe it or not, he's no different than you.

The purpose of this chapter was to help you see the other side of the picture and to influence you to stay calm in the face of obstacles. Don't take it as a self-fulfilling prophecy, for these examples may never happen to you.

Hector, age thirty, single, a bricklayer says, "I have a temper that is hard to control. It's like driving a car without brakes. Sometimes I simply can't stop, even when I want to. I lose my head. It's no different than temporary insanity. I swore that I was not going to end up like my father, letting my temper get the best of me, but I ended up in jail for fighting with a guy that made a pass at my girlfriend. I should have been flattered that he thought that I had good taste in women, but instead I felt threatened.

"I used to think that walking away from a fight was not the macho thing to do, but now I realize that it takes a bigger man to walk away than stay. I've learned that I can't tell a friend what made me angry without replaying it again in my mind and getting furious all over again. I look for a diversion. Now I go to the batting range and hit baseballs."

Ray, age seventeen, a high school dropout with an arrest record tells his story. "I was riding my friend's motorcycle around the block when a police officer stopped me. He ran the VIN (vehicle identification number), and to my surprise, the cycle was stolen. I told him that it was not my motorcycle and that it belonged to my friend who lives a block away. We went to his house and he wasn't there. I tried to explain that my friend bought it last week and didn't steal it, but that didn't matter to the officer. I told him that I wasn't going to jail for something I didn't do, and when he tried to put the handcuffs on me, I resisted. I was not only arrested for possession of a stolen vehicle but resisting arrest as well and went to juvenile home.

"I was angry with the cop, my friend, the person who sold him the motorcycle, and my parents who made me stay in juvie overnight without picking me up. I was not a thief, why did I have to pay for someone else's mistake? I alienated my parents because they didn't believe me.

"Just that one incident changed my whole outlook on life. I quit school and tried to get a job. That was a joke. The only job I could get was at the car wash. My girlfriend and I moved into a cheap studio apartment together, but we can barely pay the rent. I don't even have enough money to get an old car for transportation. Last month I found out that my girlfriend was pregnant. How am I going to pay the doctor bills? I really regret being so defensive with the cop. It wasn't his fault that I was riding a stolen cycle." Eric, age nineteen, not married, who works in lawn maintenance, says, "I can't find a decent paying job. I'd like to get married but I can barely afford gas for my car. I'm sharing an apartment with my girlfriend and another couple. One night, I had a few beers and got behind the wheel. I broadsided another car and injured two people badly. I had no car insurance since I let it lapse after the first three months so now I am responsible for their medical bills, repair of their car and I'm being sued. I went to jail and have all the fines and costs involved besides the towing charges for my car. I'll have to leave it at the impound lot because the charges are more than the car is worth. I guess I'll be eating rice and beans the rest of my life."

I have seen so much devastation from the addiction of alcohol and drugs that it brings much sadness to me. It has turned so many people's lives into a living hell. It damages their heath, emotions, spirituality, initiative, finances, family, and relationships, and gives them a police record. until they see the light, it will always be someone else's fault. That, of course, is the nature of addiction.

NOTES:

CHAPTER 10

DECISIONS

When our lives are turned upside down, we often become sick. We may get depressed or overwhelmed if we don't feel worthy, loved, or productive. Behavior doesn't cause disease, but the stresses in our life contribute to its onset. Therefore, we have some decisions to make.

First, we need to identify what's bugging us, or why we can't move ahead. Any traumatic or emotional event that happens to us is embedded in our mind. It won't go away by just talking about it. That's like putting a bandage on a splinter. The wound will become sore and fester unless we dig down deeply to get the splinter completely out. This is where hypnosis can be so helpful. It's a great tool to uncover any hurt from the past that you may have subconsciously blocked.

This hurt may have occurred while you were a child. Maybe a teacher called you stupid, or perhaps you assumed you were dumb by the grades listed on your report card. Your parents may have said you were lazy and would never amount to much. Your uncle teased you because you stuttered, and you heard your grandma tell someone that you were a hard kid to love. All these things have an impact on us. When you're hypnotized, you can find your stumbling blocks of the past and learn the reasons you built walls and barriers to shut others out. You don't lie to yourself under hypnosis. The truth is apparent.

We all make mistakes in life by doing something we later regret. Usually, it's not a mistake when you made it. It was the best you could do at that time with the information you had.

You are older and wiser now, and looking back you may have thought you did the wrong thing (and maybe you did), but how much did you know at age eleven, fifteen, or seventeen? Even if you had done things differently, there are no guarantees that things would have turned out better. Many things happen along the way that change our destiny (for better or worse).

Maybe you got behind the wheel drunk and had a wreck. That mistake taught you—or should have—that you shouldn't drink and drive. What lessons have you learned from your mistakes? If you haven't learned anything, then the mistakes will probably be repeated.

We all have our own private demons whether we are dealing with neglect, molestation, abuse, betrayal, rape, or shame. Everything has taken a toll. There are many injustices in the world, and we have caused some of them. We have done things to others that we are not proud of. It's how we grow from these mistakes that is important.

Mistakes often lead to guilt. Guilt is a learned emotional response that causes us to feel worthless and ashamed. It lowers our self-esteem. It has no value other than its own self-destruction. There are many forms of guilt resulting from criminal acts, sexual acts, inhumane acts, etc., as well as guilt from taboos and hang-ups due to various religions and cultures.

You must ask yourself what harm you are doing to yourself and others. If you feel guilty about something, then figure out a way to compensate for the mistake. Excuses don't help but deeds do.

There are ways of making amends so that you can come to terms with your guilt and move on with your life. To have an emotion of guilt is to play God. He is the only one who can sit in judgment. You can't be judge, jury, and executioner.

Overcoming your transgressions and sins are a way of growth—as long as you learn from your mistakes and don't become a repeat offender.

Consider becoming an organ donor if you have harmed someone. If you stole, reimburse your victim or give a donation to a church. If you feel that you need to give something back to the community for defacing property, then volunteer your time to a worthwhile cause.

Your motivation is to feel good about yourself, emotionally, physically, and spiritually. If any of these needs go unfulfilled, they will create a sense of frustration and imbalance. When you feel uncomfortable and displeased with yourself, you will do whatever is necessary to make yourself comfortable, even if the behavior is harmful like taking drugs, drinking, overeating, or gambling compulsively.

You may do nothing to stop yourself, because doing something takes thought and effort. If you think that you can't make the effort right now, then ask yourself when. Next week? Next year? Today truly is the first day of the rest of your life, so make up your mind now.

Decisions always involve some type of loss; that's why they're so hard to make. The past is the past and you can't change it. The most you can do is learn from it.

You may have a job you hate, a marriage that is floundering, a family relationship that is falling apart, and financial difficulties. If you don't get off your butt and get help, you are not where you want to be and not where you could be. You're simply wallowing in your misery. This makes you angry, but the evidence indicates that you would rather put things off by procrastinating than to face the problem and work to change it. Nobody said it was going to be easy. Remember, the only difference between a rut and a grave are the dimensions.

Happiness should not be contingent on external factors or circumstances. (But winning the lottery could still make me jump for joy.) Being happy and content comes from the inside out. It occurs when you take responsibility for your own behaviors and when you are pleased with who you really are, warts and all.

If you're miserable over a situation and it's going from bad to worse, it can get better *if* you do just what you have been putting off (getting a divorce, changing jobs, moving, or quitting smoking).

That's the secret, and it bears repeating; *Do what you have been putting off.*

If you're sick and tired of being sick and tired, then make up your mind to get the weight off your shoulders and relieve your frustration. This quality decision (to do something) will motivate you to become an achiever, one goal at a time. It sounds impossible, yet you know it has to be done.

Get hypnotized if you can. It will be worth the sixty dollars or so that you pay for a session. If you're broke, then you must ask a friend to help you focus on what has to be done, even if he or she has to go with you to get you started.

There are some things that just can't be put off. This is the time when you are hurting, worrying, angry, taking drugs, drinking, gambling, overeating, and confused. *Don't postpone what you need- to do.* Tomorrow may be too late to say, "I'm sorry or I love you" if there is another terrorist attack like the one of September 11, 2001. You don't want to live with regrets.

Make a promise to yourself right now, one that you know positively you can keep. Maybe it will be to do thirty jumping jacks a day, or maybe to stop your midnight snack. Do this tomorrow; then after that do it for another twenty-four hours. Keep doing it in manageable increments.

When I promised myself that I would quit smoking, it was only for a day, then a week, then a month at a time. It would have been impossible to say that I was going to quit forever. But after two weeks, I didn't want to fall back to a bad habit, so I convinced myself that I could go two more weeks, etc.

To think in terms of forever is too overwhelming. If you can't keep a promise to yourself for more than a day, then you can't grow. You will not be free until you learn to be true to yourself and accept full responsibility for your life and your needs.

You will have to accept other people's behavior without feeling that it's your job to set them straight. You need to allow them the same personal freedom that you want and expect. You can only be as compassionate and understanding of others as you are compassionate and understanding of yourself. It's not your fault that you were born into a certain set of circumstances, but it is your fault if you don't do something about it.

The difference between wanting something and getting it is taking the first step. If you're having problems getting started, then daydream about the results. Take imaginary steps and make believe that you're already there. Daydreaming gives you a head start on your goal.

If you believe in God or a higher power, don't forget the power of prayer. I get my strength from God. I carry a key chain that says WWGD (what would God do), and it is a constant reminder that if I don't know how to handle a situation, I should ask myself what He would do and follow through accordingly.

Know that there is a price for everything. If the price is not money, then it might be time or your personal freedom. You may have to give up a certain television program or stay home from a football game to complete a project. The price you pay may be giving up a relationship for financial security or emotional piece of mind. Is the price too high? Maybe a new job pays higher wages but involves much traveling and time away from the family. Is that price more than you can live with?

After you have read this book, forget about having Stimulus Overload. It is not an excuse; it is a condition. You are a unique person with certain problems, but who doesn't have problems?

I hate to be the one to tell you this, but S.O. doesn't go away. It can get better when we are not so stressed, but it won't disappear. Don't be embarrassed to get help if you need it. If you can't adopt some coping mechanisms, and you're having severe problems, seek medical help. Otherwise laugh at some of your follies and move on.

Don't forget that hypnosis can relax you and help you break bad habits, resolve past emotional issues, and allow you to focus on the future. A yoga class also works wonders in helping you relax and in calming your mind.

Move on with your life and become a productive citizen. You are no more the worse for wear. Dealing with Stimulus Overload has built character, perseverance, humility, tolerance, and a resiliency to bounce back.

WORDS OF WISDOM

People are always blaming their circumstances for what they are. I don't believe in circumstances. The people who get on in this world are the people who get up and look for the circumstances they want, and if they can't find them, make them.

—George Bernard Shaw

A journey of a thousand miles must begin in a single step.

—Lao-Tzu

The longer I live, the more I realize the impact of attitude on life. Attitude, to me, is more important than facts. It is more important than the past, than education, than money, than circumstances, than failures, than successes, than what other people think or say or do. It is more important than appearance, giftedness, or skill. It will make or break a company . . . a church . . . a home. The remarkable thing is we have a choice every day regarding the attitude we will embrace for that day. We cannot change our past . . . we cannot change the fact that people will act in a certain way We cannot change the inevitable. The only thing we can do is play on the one string we have, and that is our attitude . . . I am convinced that life is 10% what happens to me and 90% how I react to it And so it is with you . . . we are in charge of our attitudes.

—Charles Swindoll

QUESTIONS TO ASK YOURSELF

1. What would make life easier for you? (a better job, a more supportive spouse, car paid off, lawn maintenance once a week)

2. What undesirable behavior do you want to change? (anger, pouting, procrastinating, complaining, gambling, smoking, drug use)

3. What plan are you going to start working on? (twenty minutes of exercise daily, to stop smoking for a week, to lose five pounds, to clean out a cupboard)

4. What dreams are unfulfilled? (to have a child, to travel to Europe, to have a happy marriage, to go back to school)

5. What would you do if you had the day off? (go fishing; take a picnic lunch up to the mountains,

shop, spend time with a spouse)

6. Where can you go in your house or apartment to find your quiet sanctuary? (bathroom, closet, garage, patio)

7. Who are your role models today? Who were they when you were a kid? (a certain teacher, president, grandfather, Michael Jordan,

8. Tiger Woods, a popular entertainer)

9. What was the nicest thing you ever did for a relative? (change a tire, cared for him/her during an illness)

10. Who can you confide in and talk to about anything? (friend, minister, hotline)

11. If you could have any job that you wanted, what would it be? (doctor, athlete, pilot, singer, attorney, cocktail waitress)

12. If you only had six months to live, how would you spend your time? (writing letters to loved ones, bungee jumping, going somewhere exotic)

13. If you won a million dollars, how would you spend it? (buy a new house, share it with family, take a cruise)

14. . What would you like other people to say about you? (that you're: intelligent, gentle, cheerful, hard worker)

15. What is your most prized possession? (trophy, jet ski, ring, painting)

16. What would make you healthier? (take vitamins, stop smoking, exercise)

17. What can you do to be more organized? (keep a notebook handy, toss junk mail, lay out my clothes for work the night before)

18. Name two past events that had the most negative impact on your life.

19. 8. Name two past events that had the most positive impact on your life.
20. What group or club would you like to join that would reinforce your interest? (car club, weight loss group, swim team, Toastmasters)

"WHAT IF…" LISTS

Use these questions and ideas to make a cheat sheet of sorts, something to refer to when your brain is not in gear. This preparation may keep you from becoming hysterical or going ballistic with anger. I keep a tote bag on hand filled with all the necessities I'd need if I had to suddenly take someone to the hospital. I suggest you purchase a small notebook and list the things you will need for each circumstance. In each category, I have listed some questions to ask yourself as well as a few suggestions regarding necessary items.

Feel free to add to the list at any time. Make it your own.

EMERGENCY LIST HOSPITAL

Things you need to take along include: ID, insurance card(s), a magazine or book to read, pen and paper, notebook, reading glasses, snacks, bottle of water, worry beads

FUNERAL

1. What would you wear if you had a funeral to attend tomorrow? Is everything cleaned and ironed?
2. Who do you need to notify before you leave? (your boss or supervisor, other family members)

LEAVING TOWN DUE TO EMERGENCY

1. If you need to fly out of town tomorrow on an

emergency, what would you pack? Are those items clean and ready to go?

2. Do you have enough money in your wallet, or do you need to stop at the bank before you leave?

AUTOMOTIVE EMERGENCIES

1. What do you need to carry in your vehicle trunk for emergencies? (flashlight with good batteries, flares or a flasher, blanket, duct tape, water for the radiator as well as bottled water to drink, extra fuses, motor oil, jumper cables, paper towels, bungee cord)

2. What would you do if a power line fell onto your car with you in it?

3. What would you do if your car was swept away in a flash flood, and you couldn't get out?

4. What would you do if you had a wreck? (If it's minor, exchange names and get the following info: address, phone number, where the other driver works, the name of his insurance company, the name of the registered owner of the vehicle, exact address of the accident. If it's serious, call the police and advise the dispatcher of injuries, give an exact location, provide aid if necessary, write down names and license plates of witnesses, put on flashers or set out flares if there is a chance of another accident due to heavy traffic or poor visibility.)

POWER OR UTILITY OUTAGES

1. What would you do if you had a power outage for twenty- four hours or longer?

2. What would you do if the water were shut off for forty- eight hours?

WHAT TO TAKE ALONG FOR WORK OR

RECREATIONAL OUTINGS

1. What's on your checklist to take to work? (briefcase, backpack, lunch pail, wallet, keys for office, bottle of water, paperwork, jacket, necktie, padlock, cell phone)
2. What do you need to take along when you're going boating? (sunscreen or sun block, towels, blanket, money, bathing suit, thongs, life vests, bottled water, snacks, ice chest, tow rope, bumper guards, baseball cap, keys)
3. What should you take along on a picnic? (food and beverages, sunscreen or sun block, blanket to sit on, bug spray, umbrella for shade)

CONGRATULATIONS!

You finished this book,

and you thought that you couldn't finish anything!

You are on your way to a beautiful journey through life.

Live,

Love,

Laugh,

Dance,

and reach out and embrace every precious day.

For not everyone

is given the opportunity

to experience another sunrise.